Teaching Hacks!

Ideas to Make Life as a Secondary-Level Teacher Easier

By Danielle Carlson

Illustrated by Aaron Carlson

v9.30.17

Table of Contents

Preface

My first year teaching was busy and crazy. Is that really a surprise to anyone? Probably not.

While I was a confident and well-prepared first-year teacher, the year was still quite clumsy and frustrating. I remember hearing that it takes about three years for a teacher to *really* get a handle on things, and now, looking back, I'd have to agree.

During my first three years, I attended workshops, read books, and scoured the internet in a hungry search for tips and ideas to make my teaching life simpler. I stumbled upon information here and there; over the span of several years, I slowly incorporated each tidbit into what I now consider my personal arsenal of teaching hacks.

At some point, I realized that my assemblage of hacks was too useful to keep to myself. As a first-year teacher, I would have sold my soul (well, *maybe* not that far) to own such a collection of information. I figured that other young educators probably felt the same way, so I started presenting workshops to pre-service, in-service, and first-year teachers at conferences and a local educational agency. My sessions were always well-attended, and the positive feedback I received encouraged me to write this book and reach out to an even larger audience.

The ideas in this book aren't necessarily new. Some are original, but many are collected concepts from workshops, observing cooperating teachers and co-workers, and from having conversations with others in the field. What makes this book different, though, is that all the ideas are TOGETHER. What you have in your hands is not an isolated book on JUST classroom management, JUST active learning, or JUST organization. It's all those things together, and more.

If you are a veteran teacher, I encourage you to stay with me! I know it sounds like this book is only for new teachers, but I wrote this with you in mind, too. I admit that you may find some aspects less useful than others, as you are probably comfortable with how you do certain things at this point in your career. However, I know that whenever I read a new book, talk to another teacher, or flip through an educational journal, I *always* find at least one new thing to try in my classroom. Based on my experience, and with how much I have packed into this book, I have a feeling that you will find at least one new thing to try. I actually hope that you find LOTS of new things to try, but hey, one thing is better than nothing!

In this book, I will present you with tips and tricks in six areas: policies and procedures, organizing your physical space, active learning, building relationships, classroom management, and a "miscellaneous" section. I will also direct you to some of my favorite resources if you would like to do some further reading and/or exploring on your own.

It is my sincere hope that you find the items in this book useful!

A Little Bit About Me

Since we're going to hang out for awhile, let me tell you a bit about myself. I always like doing this with students, as it helps me build relationships with them. I wholeheartedly believe that solid relationships with students are the keystone to a successful classroom.

In terms of my educational background, I grew up in a Milwaukee suburb and attended a large high school with about 1,500 students. Currently, I teach in a small, rural school in Southwest Wisconsin with about 350-400 students (6th-12th grade in one building). What a culture shock! When the whole school gets together for a pep rally or assembly, I always laugh – the number of students in the *school* is roughly equal to the number of students in my *senior class*. It's a different world, for sure!

During my first year, I taught 7th grade Earth Science, 9th grade Earth Science (a trimester course), 10th grade Biology, and 11th/12th grade Anatomy & Physiology. My schedule has changed some over the years, and I no longer teach middle school. My current classes include Biology, A.P. Biology, Anatomy & Physiology, Applied STEM, Environmental Science, and an independent study research class. Yikes, right?! Good thing I love it!

On the non-educational side of things, I love spending time with my husband, Aaron, and our dog, Tessa. I enjoy gardening and being outdoors – I dream of having a hobby farm with a greenhouse and chickens. I am obsessed with sloths (they are cute, nap all day, and are experts at being non-stressed!), I enjoy strength training and yoga, traveling is my passion, I laugh at everything, and I am always mesmerized by the beauty of the ocean. Another fun fact is that I taught myself to play violin in 2012, started taking lessons in 2013 (I still take lessons to this day), and became "good" enough to play in a community orchestra. Note that I use the term "good" loosely. I'm about as good an average middle school student, and I didn't have to audition to be in the orchestra. They haven't kicked me out yet though, so that's a plus!

Enough about me—it's time to get down to business. Are you ready to make your life easier? Let's do this!

Chapter 1: Procedures and Policies

Sloth tip: *Having set procedures and policies is an important first step for running an effective classroom!*

As a student teacher, like all student teachers, I worked under the policies and procedures set by someone else. When it came time to lead my own classroom, suddenly, I had to design systems for collecting work, recording grades, weighting grades, and lots more — things I never really thought much of in the past.

If you are a new teacher, I hope to prepare you for these potentially surprising aspects of teaching. If you are a veteran teacher, you might find some new ideas to utilize in your classroom. These ideas, tips, and tricks have worked for me, and if they work for you, please use them!

Collecting Work

Did you know that organization assists with classroom management? Believe it or not, something as simple as having a set place and method for collecting work from students is an easy way to prevent classroom chaos.

Imagine that you have no set place or routine for collecting work. Students come in and you notify everyone that work is due; depending on the age group and maturity level of the students, this may lead to large amounts of wasted time. Some might come up to give you the papers, some might stay in their desks and hand the work to the end of the row, and some might start talking with their friends (ignoring you altogether). It might take you five minutes to get everything collected and everyone settled down; that's five minutes of your already-too-short class period gone.

Instead, imagine a classroom that looks like this: every day when the students walk in, they see a slide up on the projector screen telling them what is due at that very moment, what they will be doing in class, and what will be assigned as homework later. Since the students immediately know what is due, they grab their homework and take it to a bookshelf at the front of the room where work is collected, put it in the proper bin for their class, head to their seats, and get started on the first task of the day. The bell rings and the teacher announces what is due (to remind the small handful of students who never look at the board, even though it's a daily routine), a couple scrambling students grab their assignments and turn them in, and then the students continue to work on the next activity.

In case you didn't guess already, that's a snapshot of my classroom. Turning in work takes very little time, and I'm immediately able to move into the first task of the day when the bell rings because my students have been trained to follow a certain procedure. When students are trained in your procedures, they know how to do things without confusion and downtime. Confusion and downtime are often reasons why students act out, so, if order is maintained, students are denied the opportunity to cause problems. It's as easy as that!

In terms of policies for turning in work, you need to find what works for you based on your educational philosophy (do you care if something is turned in late?) and your physical space. In my classroom, I was lucky enough that the teacher before me left a great big bookshelf in the classroom. I used the bookshelf to set up my homework bins. On the shelves, I have a tray for each class, and I use a label maker to mark which tray goes with which class (see picture on next page).

After I set the physical location for collecting work, I considered my philosophy, designed a system, and trained my students to follow the system. As for my philosophy, I believe that work should be turned in on time, and late items should be separated from the pile so I remember to adjust scores accordingly later. With that in mind, I developed a procedure that works for me:

- Students turn in their work at the beginning of the class period, as explained earlier.

- I take all the on-time papers out of the bin and put them in a "To Be Graded" file folder for their class. I use colored folders and have separate colors for separate classes; for instance, all my Biology classes have red folders, and because I typically have three sections, I have three red folders labeled with the appropriate hour. My other classes have different colored folders so I can quickly see which folders are for which class.

- I put the "To Be Graded" folder on my desk so I remember to look at the papers later. I do not leave the folder where students can reach it, otherwise a sneaky student might slip their late paper in the folder while I am not looking (I saw someone do that once when I was in high school!).

- With the on-time papers removed, I know that any items that end up in the bin throughout the hour are late. When I get the chance, I write "L" at the top so I know that it's late, and I put it in the folder with the work from everyone else to grade later.

This system works very well for me, and if it works for you, use it! If not, tweak it so you have something that does work, and then train your students in your new procedure.

I start to train my students in the "collecting work" procedure on the second day of school, as soon as students have their first assignment due. I always start by reminding students to immediately look at the board and see what needs to be turned in to the bin. Then, I walk students through the rest of the process—find the work, turn it in, move on to the next task written on the board. On that second day, I also explain my late work policy — I clearly identify what I consider "late" and how I score

18

late work (more on that later). Finally, I have my students practice turning in the assignment, and then we continue through the lesson. The next day, we repeat the procedure; I give a verbal reminder to check the board, I ask if anyone has a late assignment to turn in, I collect work, and then we move on. I do this a couple of days in a row so students get used to the system, and after a short period of time, they're experts who have been trained to use the bins efficiently and without creating chaos.

Grading Work Faster

While "grading work" isn't something that has direct impact on classroom management, if you are a new teacher, there will be some things about grading work that you might not realize. Remember, I want to give you tips and tricks to make your life easier; hopefully, these tips will help you out by speeding up your grading process so you have more time to do other things!

The biggest mistake that many new teachers make when they are grading, say, a test — they check the entire test for one student, then check the entire test for another student, then check the entire test for another student, and so on. **Do not do this**. It will take you _forever_ to grade things. The secret is to ~~grade one~~ or a few questions at a time, and flip through *all* the papers, thinking about only that one question. When you get through the stack, focus on another question or two, check all those questions on all the papers, and keep repeating until you are done with the assignment.

Here is an example. Let's say that you are grading a multiple choice section of a test and the answers to the first ten questions are: A, C, C, B, A, D, B, A, C, D. Stack up all of the tests, and focus on the first three: A, C, C. Go through every single paper, keeping "A, C, C" in your mind, and marking items wrong as needed. When you get to the end of the pile, take the next section. Notice how this next section spells out the word "BAD"- because that's easy to remember, maybe you can correct five answers on your next pass through the paper stack— BAD, BA. Keep thinking "BAD BA" as you correct, make it through the stack, and start over with the next set of questions. This technique is especially helpful when grading short answer questions, as your mind is constantly on the same question, and you can really focus on one item (or a small set of items) at a time. This method also makes it easier to compare student answers and get a feel for how students are doing (who understands the concept and who does not) on a question-by-question basis.

Another grading tip is that if you decide to use word searches or crossword puzzles as assignments, you will quickly learn that they are horrible and annoying to grade with any sort of accuracy. To make grading these more tolerable, take a blank transparency paper, put it over your answer key, and circle/write in the correct answers with a transparency marker. When you correct student work, all you need to do is hold the transparency over their paper, wiggle it around a little bit to find the lines or words underneath, and voila! Done.

Recording Work

When grading work, I find it helpful to keep a spreadsheet with student names in alphabetical order within the "To Be Graded" folder for each class. Sometimes, I just input scores directly into our grade tracking program as I grade things and skip my paper spreadsheet altogether, but that's usually not the case. Most of the time, I write the scores down first—I especially go this route if I am not near a computer, or grading over a long period of time.

I like to write my scores down because backup copies are lifesavers. There have been a few times where I forgot to put a grade in the computer for a student (how does that happen?!), or I put the grade in wrong, or I accidentally delete a score from the software and hit "save" too fast. Thankfully, because of my paper grade sheet, I am almost always able to find and correct my mistake.

When I use the paper for recording grades, I have a bit of a "code" that I use to help keep track of absent students and late work (see picture on next page):

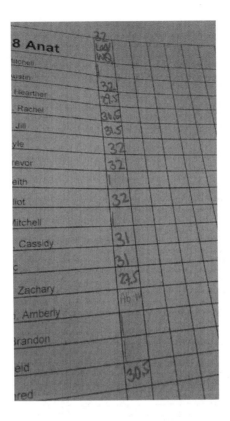

At the top of the chart, I write the name of the assignment and how many points it was worth (in the picture, it was a 32-point Lab/WebQuest). In the boxes that correspond with each student, I write the score that the student earned on the assignment. If the assignment was not turned in and will be late when it finally *is* handed in, I put a vertical bar off to the left of the box. This leaves room for me to write in the score later on, signals to me that the score isn't a zero, and also reminds me that the item is late. If a student is absent, I write "Ab" and the date that the assignment is due for him or her (check out the fourth full box from the bottom in the picture; you will see "Ab-W," which is my code for absent, due on Wednesday).

My brain is so busy every day; I know that if I don't mark down whose work is missing due to an absence and whose is simply late, I will forget when it comes time to grading the work. For instance, if Amberly turned in her late work on Thursday and I didn't make a note to myself that it was due for her Wednesday (in this case, making it only one day late), I would probably forget that she was absent altogether and mark it three days late (since the assignment was due for everyone else on Monday). However, with things properly marked on my log sheet, I would know to only mark her assignment one day late.

I also leave comments to myself like this — about absences, late work, when items are due for certain students, etc. — in the online gradebook so I have all the information in two places (on my paper sheet and online). Our program has a "comments" box near each student's assignment, which makes this very easy for me. If a student is absent, I can type "ABS" as a homework code and in the "comments" box, make note of the adjusted due date. This gives me a quick reference and a reminder when it comes to grading work, which helps me keep everything straight. I teach over 100 students every day, and this sort of "secretarial" organization ensures that I grade efficiently and consistently across all classes and for all students.

Homework Late Passes

If you have studied classroom management at all, you probably know that part of having a good system is earning the respect of the students. When students respect you, they will work for you, and they will create fewer problems overall. One way that I earn the respect of my students is by acknowledging that they lead busy lives (well…most do), and that I am willing to provide some flexibility based on this fact.

At the beginning of every quarter, I hand out a very small (the size of a business card) homework pass that looks something like this:

I change the name of the class at the top for my various classes (A&P, Bio, A.P. Bio, etc.), photocopy a bunch on colored paper (a new color each quarter- and a DARK color so students cannot photocopy and make more of their own), cut them out, and give one to each student. I tell the students to put their name and hour on the pass RIGHT AWAY so no one else can claim it, and then I tell the students to put the passes somewhere safe. I do not provide new passes if a student loses his or hers.

As the pass says, if a student comes with an unfinished assignment, the student can hand me the homework pass instead of the assignment and gain two more days to finish the work. I always make note of this on my paper grade sheet ("HWP-W" would be my code for "used homework pass- now due Wednesday") and in the "comments" section of the online gradebook. As with late and absent work, this coding reminds me not to mark work late if it is submitted within the window of extra time. It also helps me figure out how late an assignment is if it's turned in beyond the homework pass window: if the assignment was due Monday, a student uses their pass and adjusts the due date to Wednesday, but turns in the work Thursday, I'd only mark it one day late instead of three.

If a student keeps his or her homework pass all quarter and does not use it, I reward the student. She or he can turn the pass in for five extra credit points. This usually only bumps up quarter grades by a percent or less, due to the way I weight my grades (more on weights later), so it has enough of an impact to motivate students to keep the pass, but not enough to severely inflate student grades. All students receive a new pass at the start of the next quarter.

Feel free to take this idea and run with it! Copy my pass word-for-word if you would like, or change things to make it your own. Over the years, I found that students really appreciate these passes, and I love using them for the extra flexibility they provide. On a side note, if you are looking for non-food rewards for review games, good behavior, or other competitions, using bonus homework passes as prizes is a great way to provide some extra motivation. I have had success with that as well.

Absent Work

Another way to avoid possible classroom management issues is to have a solid procedure for students to pick up absent work upon their return to school. For instance, if multiple students are absent and you do not have a set procedure, you might be flooded with students coming up to you the next day asking, "What did we do yesterday? Where is my work? How do I do this?" You will waste your time—and the learning time of other students—repeating the same instructions over and over and focusing on a small subset of students rather than the whole class. If you are ignoring the rest of your class, it's a free invitation to start acting up because you're not paying attention.

I hope that by now, you are starting to see a major point- *you can prevent many classroom management issues just by having good procedures in place.*

In my classroom, I have an extra bulletin board that is called the "While You Were Out" board. Returning students are trained to grab their items off this board when they walk into my classroom. Some even get the items outside of their class time or have siblings stop by and pick up the work, and it does not disturb my class because the board is right by my door. This board is so convenient because someone can stop in, grab work from it, read the information sheet that explains what to do, and quietly leave.

My board is divided up for my four main classes, as shown in the picture:

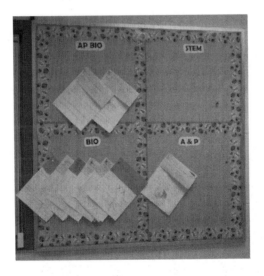

To prevent having to explain the same instructions over and over, I created a form to put on each person's work (see next page). I copy three forms per full sheet of paper.

I keep a ton of these forms, copied on bright colors and cut up, stored in a drawer that is easy to access. When a student is gone, I simply gather the work that he or she missed (plus any returned work) and staple this slip on top. I fill in the student's name, hour, what day(s) they were absent (the checkbox format works nicely if a student is gone multiple days in a row—you can just checking off the appropriate date boxes and keep adding information to the same slip), if anything is due, what we did in class, what they need to do to know about the work, and how I adjusted the due date. This leaves no question about what the student needs to do or how to go about getting it done!

It's a very slick process and I have been pleased with the results ever since I started using this system. As with the homework pass idea, feel free to copy what I do word for word, or make it your own! *I give you permission* to plagiarize my "While You Were Out" slip! Steal my ideas! I want to make your life easier, remember? Take, take, take!

Name _____ Hr _____ Absent: ☐M_____ ☐T_____ ☐W_____ ☐Th_____ ☐F_____

Before you were gone, _____ was assigned and is due <u>right now</u>!!! Turn it in!!!!

What we did in class:

_____

_____

_____

_____

What you need to do:

☐ Get the notes from someone or get them on my website,

    www.fhsmissb.weebly.com

☐ Wkst/WSQ/webquest, due on _____ for you (2 days after you come back)

☐ Take quiz, test, or do lab by _____. Please schedule a time

    with me to get this done!!!

One last thing—before I staple the papers together and tack them up on the board, I also physically write two things on all paper assignments: when the student was gone, and the adjusted due date (two days after their return). This not only helps the student keep track of new due dates, but also helps remind me about adjustments in case I forget to write the information down on my spreadsheet and/or in the gradebook (it's happened). An example of what this looks like is shown in the picture below:

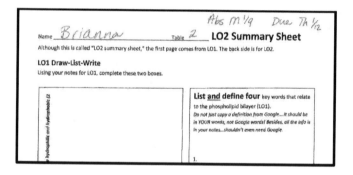

Other Homework-Related Tips

As a teacher at the secondary level, you may want to categorize and weight your grades. If you're a new teacher, you might have no idea where to start. Or, perhaps you've been teaching awhile and you want to transition to a weighted system, or you don't like the weights you're currently using. The way I weight grades obviously isn't for everyone, but it works for me, and sometimes it's just nice to see what other people do as a reference point.

In my classroom, I use the following categories and weights in my general classes (my upper level classes are slightly different), and the gradebook calculates student score appropriately:

- Daily work (10%)- things like video questions, teamwork scores, conferences, or in-class activities
- Homework (15%)
- Labs (20%)
- Minor assessments (25%)- quizzes, smaller projects, smaller assessments
- Major assessments (30%)- tests, larger projects, larger assessments

For me, I feel that this weighting system provides a fair overall grade for students. I put any extra credit in the "homework" category, which does help boost student grades, but not by crazy amounts. When semester grades are due, the gradebook calculates the semester grade as 40% 1st or 3rd quarter, 40% 2nd or 4th quarter, and 20% semester exam.

In terms of homework and assignments, I grade in various ways. ~~I grade some assignments on completion and others on accuracy~~. Generally, I grade ~~on completion~~ if the students just learned a ~~new or difficult skill~~ and are still practicing how to do or interpret the information. I don't believe in taking points off for getting things wrong when a student is just learning how to tackle something novel — I want the students to have the courage to actually *try* and see if they can get it right without fear of "ruining their grade." I score assignments on completion out of 10 points; I walk around with a notepad and a pen at the beginning of class and have students flip through the page(s) of the assignment to show me that the work is done. I scale their score out of 10 by estimating how much they have done; if a student finishes 75% of the assignment, I give them a 7.5/10. If a student finishes half or less of the assignment, I send them into the hall to work on it while I correct the work with the class. When the student finally turns in the assignment late, I only give him or her half credit (5/10).

Conversely, I grade assignments on accuracy when I believe that a student should have a grasp on the material at that time. As I mentioned earlier, I collect the work right away at the beginning of class, put it in a folder, and grade it later. Since I want students to make sure that they are actually *learning* the information, I do a variety of things with accuracy assignments:

- Sometimes when I grade assignments, I will write in the correct answers so students can better understand what was wrong and why. However, I've learned that when I hand back papers, it's important to direct student attention to my feedback. If I don't do this, about half the class will stuff the papers in the abyss of their binders or folders and never even look at my notes!

- Sometimes I do NOT write in the correct answers, but I stamp the paper with a customized self-inking stamp I designed and ordered from Amazon.com. It says, "OPTIONAL: Make corrections in a different color and turn in by tomorrow to earn back points." I made this stamp because that sentence was too long to write out on so many papers. I hand back the papers and give the students a day to correct their errors (which encourages learning) and earn points back.

- o For each correction that a student makes, I add half of the points back (so if a student lost two points on a question and corrects it, I add one point back).

- o If a student flipped two matching answers, I make them explain *why* the answers are flipped. This makes them think about it rather than just swap two letters and call it good.

- I make some worksheets "Get 100%" worksheets. For these worksheets, a student will finish the worksheet, turn it in, and I check the answers for accuracy/mark anything that is wrong. I return the sheet, and the student must keep fixing the mistakes until the worksheet is perfect. Once the student has 100%, I give her or him a completion grade of a 10/10. I love using these worksheets for key concepts in units, such as worksheets that go over important vocabulary words or foundational ideas that are important future topics, because the sheet really encourages learning.

In terms of how I grade late work for accuracy-related assignments, I have a 10% rule. If a student turns in an assignment a day late, I take 10% off from the value of the assignment. If it's two days late, I take off 20%. Three days is 30%, etc. I never allow a student to score below a 50% on an assignment due to late point deductions. For example, let's say that I have a 25-point assignment.

- Someone who turns in a perfect paper one day late would lose 10%, or 2.5 points, and get a 22.5/25.

- Someone who turns in a paper with three points off (-3) and three days late (2.5 points x 3 days = -7.5 points) would receive a 14.5/25.

- Someone who turns in a paper with seven points off (-7) and three days late (-7.5 points) would receive 10.5/25, but I don't allow him or her to score less than a 50% due to late point deductions, so I would level off the grade at a 12.5/25.

If an assignment is turned in late but on the same day that it was originally due (all the way up until the end of the school day), I only take off two points instead of 10%. I make an exception to this rule if the assignment is worth, say, only 10 points; if I took off two points for turning it in on the same day it was due, assuming no other points were lost, the student would get an 8/10. If they turned it in the next day, by my 10% rule, they would only lose one point and get a 9/10. Thus, in some cases, I must adjust so my policy is fair and makes sense. In the 10-point assignment case, I would take off only half a point for it being turned in on the same day (9.5/10) and 10% for it being turned in the next day (9/10). Keep in mind that this is my policy for work graded on accuracy. As stated earlier, for items graded on completion, late work is an automatic 5/10 no matter if it's turned in on the same day or five days late.

For all my assignments, the unit assessment (test, project, paper, etc.) marks the last day I will accept *any* missing work for the unit. After that, it's "too bad, so sad." I make this clear to students, study hall teachers, special education teachers, and parents as needed (if a student is missing many assignments and a test is coming up, I'll call home and let the parent know how many days the student has left to get credit for the items). I know some teachers will accept late work at any time during the quarter, but that policy just doesn't work for me, so I don't use it. As I keep saying, you need to find what works for you and go with it!

Hall Pass Policy

For some classes, you may never have to instill a hall pass policy. Personally, in my lower grade level classes (10th grade and below), I limit passes. I do not limit passes with my older students. I used to charge points for using passes and made it a part of student grades. However, after much reflection, I decided that a grade is there to represent academic knowledge and skills, and charging points for hall passes was not quite right. I decided to charge time instead.

For classes in which I limit passes, I allow students two "free" passes per quarter. These hall passes can be used to go to the bathroom or locker (I do not charge hall passes for getting a drink, as the water fountain is directly across from my room). After a student uses two passes, he or she can still go as many times as they need to after that—however, the student owes me five minutes for each additional pass beyond the two freebies. I always reiterate to the student that it's not "naughty detention" time and carries no negative connotation—rather, if she or he takes time away from being in my room for always forgetting a book or always wanting to use the bathroom exclusively during my class, then I will take some time away from him or her in return. Passes do not roll over, and there is no reward for keeping them; I simply start the hall passes over for all students the next quarter.

My hall passes are not physical items like my homework passes—otherwise I suspect that students would share them with each other all the time when running low. Instead, I keep track of hall passes on my seating charts, which are kept in page protectors (I discuss this in greater detail in the next chapter), using a transparency marker. I simply put a "tick mark" by the student who is utilizing a pass—it takes no time at all. I can quickly see who has used up their two passes and easily notify students when they run out.

Of course, I **never** limit the amount of hall passes for someone with a medical need. I also do not limit hall passes in my upper-level classes, as my higher-level students (who are usually in my class by choice) generally *want* to be in my class and do not like missing important information in the middle of the period.

If you instill a policy like this, you may be amazed at how many students change their minds and no longer need to go to the bathroom, and how many students miraculously find the ability to borrow a pencil from a friend instead of getting one from their locker! You exponentially increase the amount of time that students spend in your classroom by utilizing a limiting policy.

On a sidenote, I never make substitute teachers track these passes—substitute teachers have enough things to worry about. However, I do not make this information readily available to students, otherwise the students would definitely take advantage of the lapse in the system!

Work Time and Phone Policy

In this technology-inundated world, you must decide on what your work time and phone policy will look like. Your school might have a policy already set in place, or it might not. At my school, teachers are free to decide how to treat cell phones in their classrooms. Some teachers are very strict and never want to see phones out at all, whereas others don't mind, depending on the timing of usage.

In my classroom, I fall more on the liberal end of the spectrum, depending on the age of my students. When I taught middle school, I did not want students to have their phones out during class at all. My only exception was during work time. I know that some students like music while they work, and I have no problem with this (personally, I *always* have music on while I work). I told students that if they had headphones, they could listen to music at a reasonable level. If it appeared that they were texting, watching videos, or getting distracted by their device in some other way, I warned the student that I would take the device away. I found that this phone policy worked very well for my middle school students.

Today, as a high school-only teacher, I do not allow students to have phones out during lecture or group discussion. If I see it, I take it away until the end of the period (and if I have to do that multiple times in a week, I sent it to the office and the student can retrieve it at the end of the school day). However, while working on an assignment, I'm a bit more lenient and don't mind if they listen to music, text, or do whatever as they work...*as long as they are working.* If it's a chronic distraction, I give a warning before taking it away, but this sort of situation is rare in my classroom.

I know that some people will not agree with my policy at all, and that is okay — it works for me, and you need to find what works for you. That's what being a successful teacher is all about — borrowing ideas from others and synthesizing them into your own way of doing things!

Final Thoughts

Having well-defined policies and procedures will definitely help you run your classroom smoothly. When students stay busy, are well-versed and trained in your routines, and you do things in a clear, consistent manner, you potentially prevent classroom management issues before they ever happen.

I highly suggest that you communicate your policies and procedures not only to students, but also to parents/guardians, so everyone understands how your classroom works from the get-go. I always spend some time going over a syllabus in each class, and I have students and parents/guardians sign and date the form, which I keep filed away in a cabinet for the duration of the year. You will find a section of my Biology syllabus pictured on the next page.

Finally, keep in mind that students like to find loopholes in policies. Expect this to happen, especially during your first year or two if you're a new teacher, and know that *it is okay if it does*. Use such instances as learning experiences and improve the policies for the future. Be willing to admit your mistakes, and don't be afraid to do that in front of students if the mistake relates to them. Students like to see that you are human, too, and that you make mistakes like they do!

Welcome to **your** class! **TOGETHER**, we will explore more than just sci
you to enter the world as a thinking, learning, intelligent **adult**. I a
your **life** and the world around you. Prepar

My "rule": If you make it so I can't teach effectively or you or other students can

Consequences: Will be given in this order, except in severe cases:
- Warning
- Detention with me
- Detention in office

Materials:
- 3-ring binder or folder with pockets
- Planner- you will not be able to go ANYWHERE without it!
- Pens/pencils
- Textbook (you will have a shelf to keep it on in my room)

Optional Materials (my classroom wishlist!)
- Pump hand soap
- Cleaning wipes
- Small prizes for review games and activities

Grading:
- Categories: Daily work (10%), homework (15%), labs (20%), minor assessments (25%), major asmts. (30%)
- A=90-100   B=80-89   C=70-79
  D=60-69   F=<59 (but nobody should get one!!!)

Turning Work In: Work is due immediately after the bell rings- if it's not in, it v
turned in the same day, it is -2 points. However, each day it is turned in late beyo
value (down to a 50% on the assignment). *No late assignments will be accepted a*

Homework Late Passes: You get one late pass per quarter that can be used to ext
Lost passes will not be replaced! If you don't use it, you may save it for 5 pts eac

Absent Work: You are responsible for figuring out what you missed- I will not h
area and/or the calendar on my website. All work, labs, conferences, quizzes, tests
If it was assigned before you were gone, it's still due when you come back!!!

Extra Credit: I do not give it out freely because I believe that you need to earn y
know that sometimes you may do poorly on a test or some assignment for various
also allow you to correct most assignments since learning coincides with correctin

Tardiness: Every 3 tardies (unexcused) means you'll have a 15-minute detention

Chapter 2: Organizing Your Physical Space

Sloth tip: *Physical organization of the classroom, along with organized policies and procedures, makes classroom management easier!*

Physical arrangement of the classroom includes more than just how the desks are arranged. Here are some other ways to organize various aspects your classroom — and believe it or not, these things can help you with classroom management (more on that in Chapter 5)!

A Posted Schedule/Agenda

Many students like to know what's going on for the week in their classes. If you are in your first year, it might be difficult to plan an entire week ahead of time, but if you can, it's extremely helpful. I have a designated area of my white board reserved for my weekly schedule. Check out my photo on the next page.

I used blue painter's tape to mark the boundaries of each class (it's easier to peel off at the end of the year as compared to masking tape). The class headings/dates always stay the same and I never erase them. I use red marker to indicate what is due, black to indicate what will be done in class, and blue to indicate homework. I take a picture of the board each week and put it on my classroom website so that students can find the schedule there, too. I see students looking at this schedule often, so I know they find it useful. I also find it useful for myself when a student tells me they will be absent and requests work ahead of time—I don't have to pull out my lesson plan book to find the information. I can simply turn around and look at the board behind me!

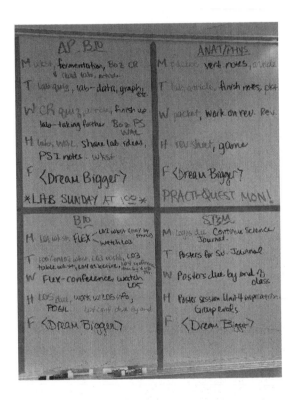

Extra Copies

You will probably always have that type of student who loses their copy of the assignment and comes in to interrupt you during another class to get a new copy. This is a classroom management issue because it provides a window of opportunity while a visitor holds your attention. If you train your students well, and if they know where to find new copies of items, this distraction will never happen!

I keep a crate with colored hanging file folders of "extras" on a side table near my "While You Were Out" board:

I always make a few extra copies of assignments; after I have passed all the papers out, I immediately put the extras in my extras bin. My students know to go directly to this bin and find the folder for their class when they need a new copy of an assignment. I often see students pop in during other classes, silently head over to the folder, pull out what they need, and leave. They never disturb my class at all!

I also post digital copies of all assignments on my classroom website, and I frequently refer to this fact throughout the school year so students remember. I am always very proud of students who are absent, know what was assigned (because they check the weekly schedule on my classroom website), print the work at home, and come with it done. There are definitely some very responsible students out there!

Tag Your Drawers

There are some materials that I keep in my drawers so that students do not randomly take items and play with them—tape, paperclips, rubber bands, etc. However, sometimes students need these items, and if I'm across the room, it can be difficult to verbally describe the location of the item. For some people, this might not be an issue, but in my classroom, I have a lot of drawers and it can be confusing (and long-winded) to say, "In the series of long drawers, go to the second one down, and look inside, off to the right." That might not sound *too* horrible, but when the student goes for the wrong drawer and you have to say, "No, down one. Down another. No, not that one. Over one," it gets really time-consuming and annoying. To solve this problem, I put different colored sticky notes on my most commonly-needed drawers:

If your picture is in black and white, all you need to know is that each drawer has a sticky note square that is a different color. Using this system, when a student needs tape, I can simply say, "Go into the drawer marked with the yellow tag and look to the right," and they know exactly where to go. It's that simple.

I also suggest heading to the dollar store and picking up some inexpensive baskets/organizers. This makes it easier for you, substitute teachers, and students to find items in drawers quickly. Here is a picture inside one of my drawers:

Rubber stamps, permanent markers, highlighters transparency markers, tape — everything has a place. You can see that my tape rolls are a bit unruly (they don't fit in the drawer well unless I spread them out), but overall, this organization keeps items findable and ready for use on a whim.

In other areas of my room, like my back laboratory area, I use a label maker to indicate what's in the various cabinets/drawers (see below). This is more for myself than for students — my room is quite large, and I often forget what I put where! My label maker saves me minutes of aimless wandering around the room, trying to find the item I need.

Paper/Mail Sorters

Mail sorters are awesome for keeping track of copies of papers that you don't need right now, but plan to use later. It might not be feasible if you're in your first year and barely feel ready for the next day, but you'll probably find it advantageous to copy papers ahead of time and have them ready to go as needed. I tend to copy an entire unit's worth of papers before my units even start (apologies to the people who have to wait for the copier when I'm down there hogging the machine). I have separate areas for my four classes in my mail sorters (I actually have two side-by-side in the picture coming up) and put my papers in the slots in the order that I use them:

Every couple days, I move the sets of papers up to fill the gaps at the top, and then I can copy the next set to fill the spaces at the bottom.

This is another organizational skill that doubles as a classroom management technique. Sometimes a lesson will take less time than you expect, and you will find yourself with 20 minutes to kill. If you have nothing ready to go, you are opening up 20 minutes of potential chaos. Conversely, if you have items for future lessons ready to go, you might be able to pull an assignment out of your sorter and start it early. Keeping students busy prevents acting out.

Salvage Furniture and Containers!

If you're at a garage sale and find an inexpensive bookshelf or file cabinet, or you have some old items at home that you never use, take them to school! I had an old bookshelf at home that I repurposed for student convenience:

On this bookshelf, students have easy access to many things, and they never need my permission to use the items located there. On the top shelf, students can find different kinds of paper (scrap, plain, colored, graph) in the trays at the top. I use the six crates next to the green trays for my six groups of tables; they have sticky notes, tape, scissors, and glue sticks in them. When we do projects that utilize those materials, I can quickly throw crates on the desk with all those items "bundled" together, instead of setting out those items one-by-one.

On the first and second shelves at the top, I utilize dollar-store baskets and more crates to store rulers, scissors, glue sticks, protractors, glue bottles, "fun" scissors, calculators, and hot glue guns. The third shelf houses colored pencils, crayons, and markers (most of those boxes are not on the shelf in this picture — they were being used by students that day!). The bottom shelf holds some odd-looking and irregularly-shaped objects, which are student-made "garbage cans" (more on that later).

I also suggest that you keep random containers that you would normally throw away or recycle at home. I have a cabinet full of yogurt containers, pie tins, take-out boxes, egg cartons, parmesan cheese containers, and more:

These items may be the most helpful when you least expect it! My random assortment of containers helped me many times during student projects and hands-on tasks; you never quite know when you're going to be interrupted by the bell, and you need a quick way to bundle each group's work before they leave. It's a lot easier to throw things in a container rather than carry everything piece-by-piece to a storage area!

Table Top Trash Cans

When I used Interactive Notebooks one year, I had students cutting up papers on a daily basis to tape into their notebooks. Consequently, this led to tons of paper scraps EVERYWHERE.

To minimize the scrap paper mess and to speed up the scrap-removal process, I decided to create table top trash cans. However, I didn't want to spend the time making them myself, so I assigned the task to one of my classes. Students were required to make a tabletop trash can small enough to fit on the desk, sturdy enough to hold scraps, and it had to be creative (not just a box they found in the recycling bin). I made it a contest (for a little extra motivation) and ended up with so many neat creations, like these:

If you do a lot of cut-and-paste work in your classroom, having students make trash cans of their own is a super useful idea! Students will love making them, and they will love using them, too. My students were trained to grab a trash can as soon as they walked in the door, and it became a race of sorts to get the "best" one first.

Hanging Table Numbers

Above my six groups of tables, I laminated and hung a number from the ceiling, one through six. I also labeled my back lab tables in a similar fashion:

Doing this made two things much easier: handing back graded papers, and assigning people to tables for group work ("You four, head to table six!").

To quickly hand back papers, I put a line for students to indicate the table they sit at (instead of their hour or class period), as shown below:

This system *really* makes a difference in how fast I can hand work back to students. After I grade an assignment, I sort all the papers by table number. I keep paper trays for each class on my desk, which are used solely to hold two things: to house work to return to students, and to keep the papers I need for that particular class that day within reach. I find the proper "Return Work to Students" folder and add the proper graded papers (note the file folders sticking out under the stacks of papers):

Before class starts, in our three-minute passing period, I can easily access the work to return to the upcoming class by finding the correct tray and locating the correct "Return Work to Students" folder. Then, because the work is already sorted into piles by table number, I can quickly walk around the room, drop off all papers at each table "pod," and let the students sort out whose is whose. It takes less than a minute!

I do not do this "drop off" method with quizzes and tests, but I still keep quizzes and tests sorted by table because it means less bouncing around the room, trying to find each student individually.

I don't know why it took me seven years to figure out this hack!!! I wish I thought of it sooner because it has been one of the biggest time-savers I've come across.

Seating Chart and Tracking Absences

Something that makes life easier for both myself and my substitute teachers is putting my seating charts in page protectors and keeping track of absences in an assignment notebook:

Having a seating chart like this makes it easy and fast to take attendance, as you get a quick visual check of who is in their spot and who is not. The page protectors are nice because they keep your seating charts clean and make the pages last longer. They are also nice because you can write on them. As explained earlier, I keep track of how many hall passes my students utilize by putting a "tick mark" directly by their name using a transparency marker.

To create my seating chart, I took a series of page protectors and held them together with two loose leaf binder rings, making it easy to flip the pages between classes. I went on my computer and printed out the design of my classroom, making lots of copies, and then wrote students' names in pencil on the sheets. This setup makes it easy to make quick adjustments as needed (for instance, if a student enters or joins a class) and to change the arrangement of students each quarter; I just slide out the old pages and insert the updated pages.

I keep an assignment notebook next to my seating chart so I can write down student absences. This helps me keep track of who is gone a lot (in case I need to discuss the matter with a parent), it makes it simpler to determine when absent work is due (in case I forget to mark it in my gradebook or on a student's assignment), and makes it easier for me to know who was gone on a day I'm not at school/to determine who I need to put work up for on the "While You Were Out" board when I return.

Create a Website

I find that maintaining a class website is one of the very best ways to communicate information to students, parents/guardians, and other people within school (such as the special education department and tutors). I particularly work to maintain a section called "This Week," where people can find the weekly schedule for my classes. I also work to maintain a page for each class that I teach (full of hyperlinks to websites that we use, links to assignments, practice tests, and more).

There are tons of simple platforms out there to get you started on creating a class website, if you do not have one already. Just do a quick search, and you will find endless options! If you want to explore my classroom website for some ideas, feel free to visit it at *www.fhsmissb.weebly.com.*

Final Thoughts

Whew, there was a lot in this chapter! Let me do a quick recap.

Simple tricks such as tagging your drawers and saving random containers make it easier for you and students to quickly find or store items. Any extra furniture that you can salvage, like filing cabinets or bookshelves, is helpful for organizing your physical space. Having an organized space saves you time and can prevent classroom management issues, as you've seen here and will read more about in Chapter 5.

Having a posted schedule/agenda helps you stay on track and provides some visual structure that many students prefer. Keeping a couple extra copies of assignments on-hand in an organized, easy-to-access area minimizes student interruptions, especially if you can "train" students to grab extra copies as they need them. Having digital copies is also helpful; this allows students to access assignments at home as needed.

Using table numbers makes it simpler to assign students to groups and to help students quickly transition to a different area with minimal confusion. Table numbers also make handing back work more efficient.

Keeping copies of future assignments in a ready-to-go location is helpful in case a lesson runs short and you quickly need something to keep students busy. Having future assignments copied and ready to go is also helpful for the times when students notify you of an upcoming planned absence; you can quickly find and give students their future homework without having to think too much about printing the assignment(s). Tracking absences is useful for keeping track of when work is due or late for students who were absent when it was assigned, and it also helps you keep track of patterns in case you need to talk with a parent or guardian about student attendance in your class.

Quite simply...organization rocks!

Chapter 3: Keep Learning Active

Sloth tip: *nobody wants to sit through 45 minutes of lecture. By constantly changing daily routines, you keep students interested and engaged!*

Ask yourself—would *you* want to sit through 45 minutes (or however long your class periods are) of your own class? Do you lecture notes all hour, or do you vary things and keep it interesting? Variety is key. Variety keeps students engaged, and when they are engaged, they cause fewer problems. From my experience, I've noticed that sheer boredom is a major reason why students act out—they have nothing better to do, so why not? For some students, being sassy is more interesting than being bored!

I teach high school science. While I wish there were days I could teach without lecturing, sometimes it's just not possible. On days when I do lectures, I make sure to keep the learning as active and engaging as possible. I also try to utilize non-lecture activities as often as I can to keep things more interesting and to break up strings of days with lectures. Here are some of the tools I utilize to keep learning active in my classroom.

Be Ready to Answer!

If you have experienced learning via lecture in the past, which you likely have, you probably know that it's hard to absorb all the information thrown at you. If you are not given the chance to process and work with the information, most of it will not stick.

As I mentioned earlier, there are times where I just cannot get around lecturing in my classes (especially in subjects like Anatomy & Physiology). To break up lectures into manageable chunks, and to force my students to summarize, think about, and work with the information presented, I throw in "Be Ready to Answer!" (BRTA) questions throughout my slideshows.

My BRTA questions vary from quick recall questions to more difficult application questions. I give the students a few minutes to work with their notes and with each other to answer the questions. Again, this gives the students the chance to process what they just learned, which helps increase engagement (and therefore understanding) throughout the lesson. See the example below:

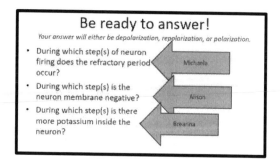

Students know that they need to attempt to answer the questions during the "work time" because I might call on them to provide an answer, and who likes being caught off guard, not paying attention, without an answer to give?!

I randomly call on students to provide answers in one of two ways. The first way takes a bit of preparation before class begins—I choose student names and put them on arrows that are hidden when the slideshow is in "presentation" mode. When I am ready for students to share answers, I simply click and the arrow with their name animates in and appears (as shown on the previous image). I keep track of who is used to make sure I am randomly rotating through all my students equally. Again, this takes some before-class preparation, but the student anticipation of possibly seeing their name on the screen and having to answer encourages students to pay more attention and work to understand the information better.

The second way I approach BRTA questions, and the format I've used more often because it takes less preparation time, is to make popsicle sticks with the students' names on them. I present the BRTA questions in the same way as before, but I randomly choose popsicle sticks to have students answer the questions. When I click on my BRTA slide, the answers to the questions appear with each click (rather than a student name- see the next image). In addition to requiring less preparation time, this version allows students taking notes at home (if they are absent) to immediately check their BRTA answers and gather instant feedback about their answers.

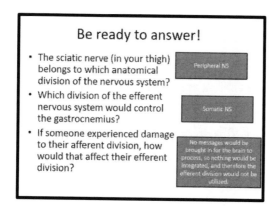

In addition to having the BRTA answers on the board, I make sure that the corresponding BRTA questions are printed in the students' note packets, too. This allows students to write out their answers, which helps some process and remember the information better. It also allows students to use the BRTA questions (with the correct answers) as a study aid for the test at the end of the unit.

```
    o   Relationship with hypothalamus
        •   Hypothalamus sends releasing or inhibiting hormones into th
        •   Causes a response in the pituitary

    Be ready to answer!
        •   If the hypothalamus sends out Prolactin Releasing Factor (PRH), what does the pituita
        •   If the hypothalamus sends out GH-IH, what does the pituitary gland do?
        •   If the hypothalamus sends out TRH, what does the thyroid gland eventually end up d


    •   ANTERIOR PITUITARY HORMONES   --WE WILL DO THIS PART IN CLASS. YOU C
        o   _____
            •   General metabolic hormone
                •   _____: amino acids used to build
            •   Causes fats to be

            •   Stimulates _____ in most target cells
```

Turn and Talk

If I feel like a lecture is getting long and I do not have a set of BRTA questions thrown in to break up the information (or I just want to change things up), I might utilize a "Turn and Talk" or "Stop and Discuss" activity. I will find a natural place to pause and ask students to turn to their neighbors and take turns summarizing what we just learned in the most recent section(s) of the notes.

Sometimes I even tell the students to quiz each other — I'll say something random like, "The person with the longest hair quizzes their partner about the first section, and the person with the shorter hair will ask questions about the second section." These quick "brain breaks," like BRTA questions, allow students to talk about and process information, making passive lecture much more engaging and easier to digest and remember. Here is an example of a simple "Turn and Talk" I use in Anatomy:

TURN AND TALK

- Identify these structures on one of your nails
  - Cuticle
  - Free edge
  - Lunula
  - Nail body/plate
- Then turn to the person next to you and identify the structures on their nail

If you wanted to bring a bit more action to your "Turn and Talk" or "Stop and Discuss" activities, you could have students get up and find a random partner somewhere around the room. I used to do this with my middle school students all the time; I'd say something like, "Find someone with the same color socks as you," or something else totally random to pair students up. Then, I'd have the students get up, find their partner, and talk about their notes for a couple minutes before sitting down. Younger students aren't built to sit in chairs all day long, so giving them a chance to get up and move is very helpful. Older students aren't really built to sit in chairs all day either, making this tactic quite useful at all grade levels!

Brainstorm Boxes, Thinkspaces, and Summary Boxes

Other ways to break up lecture include Brainstorm Boxes, "Thinkspaces," and Summary Boxes. These are just fancy titles that I use to indicate a time to think and break up the notes into smaller segments. I use Brainstorm Boxes towards the beginning of notes to see what students know:

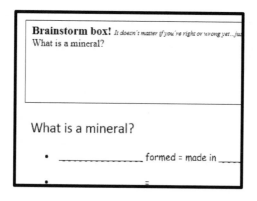

I use "Thinkspaces" to have students take their understanding of a concept a bit farther:

What is a mineral?

- _____ formed = made in _____

- _____ = _____

- _____ = not _____ or _____

- Definite _____ structure = _____ stack in a specific

- Different from a _____

  o Minerals are the _____ of rocks!

  Thinkspace!

  A mineral is NOT...

  A mineral is NOT...

And I use "Summary Boxes" to help students wrap up ideas at the end of a set of notes:

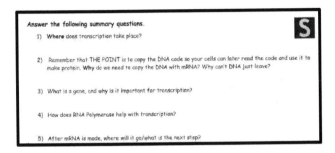

Answer the following summary questions. **S**

1) **Where** does transcription take place?

2) Remember that THE POINT is to copy the DNA code so your cells can later read the code and use it to make protein. **Why** do we need to copy the DNA with mRNA? Why can't DNA just leave?

3) What is a gene, and why is it important for transcription?

4) How does RNA Polymerase help with transcription?

5) After mRNA is made, where will it go/what is the next step?

Group Work and "Stoplights"

Utilizing group work to promote learning is a great way to keep learning active and different. However, group work can quickly get out of control if you are not taking preventative measures to make sure that groups run smoothly.

When my students complete group work, I let them choose (or sometimes I assign) roles. It might seem a bit childish, but when each person has a job that forces him or her to participate and do something active, it makes the group run more efficiently and gives students responsibility.

I always have one or two students serve as a *reader* to read information aloud to the group (one student if it's a small group of three; two students alternate in this role in a group of four); one student serves as a *reporter* and is the only group member who shares information with me when I ask for answers from the group; and finally, one student serves as the *manager/cup keeper* and makes sure everyone is on track, keeps an eye on the time, and is in charge of the "stoplight" system. With explicit, active, clearly-defined jobs, I find that group work runs much more smoothly in my classroom as compared to the way I facilitated group work in the past.

The use of the aforementioned "stoplight" system has also been critical for smooth, less chaotic group work. Stoplights consist of three different colored cups, as shown on the next page (if your image is in black and white, the top cap is green, the middle cap is yellow, and the bottom cap is red):

These cups help me quickly get a sense of how students are doing while working in their groups. Each group must keep their stoplight in the middle of their table/desk so it is easy to view from anywhere in the classroom. Then, all I have to do is glance around the room and make note of which color cup is on top. When the green cup is on top, I know that the group is working fine and has no problems. When the yellow cup is on top, they have a question (but they keep working ahead until I can get to their group). When the red cup is on top, they have finished the assigned activity and are ready for me to come over and check their answers.

I admit that I did not create the "stoplight" idea —
I heard about it from somewhere else — so kudos to the
genius who designed it! It's so easy to see where students
are at in their work, and it prevents shouting, raising
hands, and chaos!

I found small condiment storage containers
(conveniently with green/yellow/red caps!!!) at my local
dollar store to serve as my stoplights. You could easily
paint blocks or plastic cups with stoplight colors, or get
creative in other ways. You could even pose the idea to
students and challenge *them* to brainstorm objects that
you could use or build, have the students share their ideas
with the class, vote on an idea, and have each group make
a set for your class based on the winning design (sort of
how I did with the table top trash cans). Just like that, you
have an engineering lesson, and you also get a nice
product as a result. Fantastic!

Colored Index Cards

POGY Cards, as I call them, are a great way for
students to quickly review information and for you to get
a quick visual of student understanding. POGY questions
can be used as a warm-up, throughout a lecture, or as a
summary activity at the end.

POGY Cards serve as the "less technical" version of student response systems. All you need to purchase are neon-colored pink, orange, green, and yellow index cards, laminate them for durability, and create a series of multiple choice questions for students to answer. In lieu of A/B/C/D answers, answer choices are now pink, orange, green, or yellow (P/O/G/Y). I create a slideshow with a series of questions and set some sort of picture or animation to pop up and mark the correct answer at the right time (like the monkey in the picture below):

The type of epithelium found in areas that undergo lots of stretching:

- P: columnar

- O: ciliated

- G: transitional

- Y: pseudostratified

In my classroom, I put up the question and tell students NOT to hold up their answer right away — I tell them that I will ask for answers in about 30 seconds. The reason I do this is because 1) students need time to think, and 2) if six students hold up the yellow card right away, chances are that others will also hold up yellow because it's the popular answer. I tell students that they can hide their answers from others by putting other colored cards behind their answer, or by holding it in front of their body instead of up in the air (many students are afraid of getting the answer wrong and looking "dumb" in front of others). I just need to be able to see each person's final answer choice!

When ready, I ask students to show me their answers; they hold up their cards and I get a quick visual of who gets the information and who doesn't. Also, POGY cards help me see when the same incorrect answer tricks a lot of students simultaneously, giving me the chance to probe for the reason of their confusion. Did I teach the information poorly? Did I word the question wrong? Are students really lost, and I need to re-teach? POGY cards can be incredibly valuable tools, and they cost next-to-nothing.

Note that if you have any color blind students, you can write the letters (P, O, G, Y) on the cards to help them out.

Review Games

Review games are a great way to go over information in an exciting, interesting way. I use review games at the ends of my units, but you can use them at any time to "spice" things up, bring in some variety, or even kill some time if you know that your lesson will run short. Before playing review games, you need to ask yourself the following questions:

- Can your students handle competition?
- Will students be motivated to play if there is no "reward" at the end?
- If you offer a reward, what will it be?
- What will you do about students who refuse to play?
- How will you keep the "smartest" students from winning all the time and discouraging others from even trying?

Once you answer these questions, you can decide if review games will work for you, and which you would like to use.

All my classes follow the same general format when assessed by a test at the end of a unit. After we spend however many days learning the unit concepts, I give students a full class period to work on their review sheet. The next day, the review is due (graded on completion) and we correct it in class. After correcting the review, we play a review game for the rest of the class period. The following day, the students take the test.

In my classes, winning the review game is always worth extra credit on the test. All of the members of the winning team earn two extra credit points added to their test score—as long as they participate in the game. If someone refuses to play (which actually rarely happens) and their team wins, the non-participant earns no extra credit. I find that two points provides enough of a motivation for students to play and want to win while not over-inflating test grades.

I use games and grouping techniques in a way that allows all students to have an equal chance at winning. For instance, if I use a game like Jeopardy (which relies heavily on content knowledge and the stronger students usually dominate), I will design groups so that the weaker students are evenly dispersed among stronger students. If I use my favorite game, "Will the Winners Lose?", winning the game is entirely up to chance, so I am able to randomly create groups using a popsicle stick names or an online grouping tool.

I actually don't use Jeopardy as a review game anymore (it's too overused!); instead, I rotate between my three favorite games:

- **The Whiteboard Game** (simple/takes essentially no planning time): Group students into fours and give each group a whiteboard, a marker, and a tissue (for erasing). Have them choose a group name related to the unit you are studying and write the group names on the board. Create your own review questions on the fly, prepare some in advance, or have students write them for you before beginning the game. Ask the first question; to answer, a group member needs to write the answer and then hold the board up so you can see their response. The first group with the correct answer gets two points (tally scores by the group names on the main board), and everyone else, assuming they are correct, gets one point. I force groups to switch their writers each time so the fastest person cannot take over during every round. I allow students to use their notes. I DO NOT allow students to re-answer a question if they are wrong, unless EVERYONE gets it wrong. Near the end of class, I let students wager their points (like on Jeopardy) for a final question (they cannot use notes on the final question). If they get the question correct, they earn the points they wagered; if not, they lose those points. The winning team is the one with the most points at the end of the game.

The Whiteboard Game is a great one to play at the spur-of-the-moment. It takes pretty much no planning time (as long as you can come up with review questions on the fly) and is a nice way to fill some time if a lesson is running shorter than expected.

- **Grudge Ball** (moderate/takes a little more planning time): I learned about Grudge Ball, which my students refer to as "The Basketball Game," from a blog called "To Engage Them All" (Google the blog and the game, and you'll find it!). I modified some of the rules to make the game a bit more fair—as written, I found that it was too easy for a team to get "knocked out" of the competition for the rest of the class period. This made students give up hope and not care about the game anymore. This game takes a bit more work to set up as you have to put up a toy basketball hoop (I don't leave mine set up all the time, otherwise students mess with it), draw a bunch of "X's" on the board, and have questions ready (or have students create them). It also takes a bit longer than 10 minutes to get into a good game, so it's not as good on the fly. It's a ton of fun, though. Check out the blog for the rules and adapt your games as needed!

- **Will the Winners Lose?** (moderate/takes a little more planning time): I learned about "Will the Winners Lose?" from *www.EducationWorld.com* (Google "Education World" and the game title, and you'll find it!) and, like Grudge Ball, I have modified aspects of the game to make it my own. My favorite part about the game is that just because a team is answering questions correctly, it does not mean that they will win the game — it all depends on the cards that are drawn. This really gives *all* students, high or low, the chance to win the game and earn some extra credit on their test. For this game, my students write the questions for me—two questions with their answers—on index cards before we begin. I use their questions (plus some of my own) to ask the students in a "trivia style" competition. Each team (I usually play with three or four teams) sends a person up to a bell (like you'd find on a hotel desk), and the first person to ring gets the opportunity to answer the question. If the question is answered correctly, the student can choose to take a card (or not); the card is the only way that points are earned (or lost—not all of the cards are good, which is why some groups refuse to take cards when they're ahead!).

Check out the site for more information about the game and what to put on the cards. I've spiced up my deck of cards by adding a wider variety of card types. In addition to gaining points (as you'll see on the website if you check it out), my cards make students: lose points, put a negative sign in front of their score, lose all their points and go to zero, switch their score from negative to positive or vice versa, have "battle" questions against a person of their choice, switch scores with another team, win a "jackpot" of extra points (and the jackpot increases in value with every question that gets answered incorrectly throughout the game), and more. It's exciting and fast-paced, and students always choose this as their favorite review game and want to play it the most often.

Final Thoughts

As stated earlier, the key to keeping students engaged is *variety*. When students are actively engaged, they are not bored. If they are not bored, they are less likely to act out and cause problems.

There are tons of books out there, each loaded with ideas for active learning strategies. My favorite is Active Learning: 101 Strategies to Teach Any Subject by Mel Silberman. A quick Google search for "active learning strategies" will also help you find ideas for free.

Just keep asking yourself — would YOU want to be a student in your classroom? If the answer is "no," how can you make your classroom a better learning environment? There are tons of resources out there to help you out — go find some! If you don't know where to start, check out the "Resources" section at the end of my book.

Chapter 4: Building Relationships

Sloth tip: Forming solid relationships with students makes EVERYTHING easier.

Why You Need to Build Relationships

Building relationships is probably THE MOST important thing you can do in your classroom to assist with classroom management. When you get to know your students, and you let them get to know you, students are more likely to feel safe around you because they feel cared for, trusted, and respected. Safe environments encourage participation, cooperation, and conversation. If students fear you or are uncomfortable in their environment, defense mechanisms may kick in, and issues will likely occur. Some students might shut down completely, whereas others might act out.

The best way to build relationships with students is to have conversations with them — and not just school-related conversations about homework, work ethic, and/or discipline. Have conversations about sports, family, vacations, pets, hopes and dreams...the options are endless! Some lucky people are naturals at doing this and can engage even the quietest person in a dialogue. Other less fortunate people (like me) need some help making conversation. I use the following techniques to boost my conversational skills with students so I can really get to know them beyond the 45-minute snapshot I see in my classroom every day.

Beginning-of-the-Year Survey

Handing out a simple survey at the beginning of the year is one of the easiest ways to get to know students. I like asking questions about academic and non-academic things. I emphasize to students that if any question makes them feel uncomfortable, they do not have to answer it. Some sample questions and "finish the sentence" statements I include are:

- Think of one challenge you experienced last year related to school. What can you do this year to avoid facing the same issues again?
- I am afraid of…
- I am amazing at…
- Setting goals is very important, especially for accomplishing your dreams!!! There are lots of different kinds of goals — academic, social, physical, etc. Tell me — what is one goal for your life in the future?
- Tell me something random about you!

I type everything up into a simple page and hand it out on the first day of school (it's the very first assignment of the school year!).

The key to making the most of these surveys is _not to read them right away if you are still learning student names_. If you read these as students turn them in, but you really don't know who the students are yet, the information you read will get lost (unless you have a photogenic memory, perhaps) because you have very little knowledge about the student to "hook" what you've learned to that student's image and personality.

I suggest waiting a week or two after meeting new students to really dig through these surveys. My favorite thing to do is give the students work time, and as they work, choose a few surveys to read. As I read, I wander over to the selected students as they work, and I try to start up a conversation based on something I read on their sheet. For example, I might say something like, "Emma, I read your 'Getting to Know You' survey, and I thought it was so neat that you have so many horses! I grew up in the city, so I've never seen a horse up close, besides at the zoo. What is your favorite thing about horses? You could teach me so much about them!"

Over the course of a week or so, I make it around to each student and have a personal conversation with them. By doing this, I basically acknowledge that I read their sheets and that I'm interested in their lives. It's a win-win situation because I learn more about my students in the process!

Many students love talking about themselves, and you might be able to build some great foundations with students (with minimal effort!) using this method. Other students might take more time – they might only respond to your conversation starter with a word or two, and that's okay. Respect their need for space and time, and try again in the future. Everyone comes from a different background and has different life experiences; some students might take to you right away, whereas others may need a long time to trust you and feel that they can open up even the smallest amount. Just remember that expressing interest in student lives shows that you care, and that's where I like to start.

After using the sheets to get to know my students during the first couple weeks of school, I alphabetize the sheets by name and put them in my filing cabinet. As the year continues, if I have a student who is hard to reach, is a behavior problem, or I feel like I don't know the student well enough, I pull their sheet out. I find something new to talk about and try to have a conversation with the student and get to know them better. I try to show the student that I care and want to see them as a *person*, not just another kid who walks through my door. It makes a huge difference in my classroom, and I bet it will in yours, too.

At the end of the school year, I hand the sheets back to my students. They always get a kick out of what they wrote nine months before!

Random Question!

Another fun way to have conversations with students is by putting a random question on every homework assignment. I used to only do this with my 7th grade students, but I recently started adding random questions to my Anatomy & Physiology assignments (11th and 12th graders), and they loved it just as much as my middle school students.

It's as simple as it sounds—find space on your assignments and put a random question on it. I usually put mine at the bottom of the last page of the assignment, but sometimes they might end up off to the side of an assignment (basically, they go wherever I have room!). I often put the question in a different font or enclose it in a box to set it apart from the rest of the assignment. Like always, I tell students that they do not have to answer the question if they don't want to, but almost everyone does almost all the time! Here are some examples:

- What is your favorite type of sauce to put on food or dip?
- What is your favorite emoji? Illustrate or explain.
- What kind of milk do you prefer? Skim, 1%, 2%, whole, or some other form of milk?

When I grade papers, I always acknowledge the responses so the students know I read each and every one. Sometimes I might just put a quick smiley face by the answer, or I might actually write something back. It's not uncommon for a student to ask the random question back to me in class—"What's *your* favorite sauce to put on food?" and start a conversation with me (and sometimes even the whole class for a couple minutes). Again, it's so simple, but the students love it. Every once in awhile, I'll forget to put a question on a worksheet, and the students loudly lament its absence!

The hardest part is finding enough questions to make it through the year while avoiding repeats. I went to Google and searched for "random questions to ask people" and found many ideas by browsing websites, which definitely helped me find some good ideas. Additionally, I asked students to write questions that they wanted to see as random questions, and I used some of their ideas (which they really like—they brag to everyone that they wrote it!).

Another fun thing to do is turn the tables and make this your random question every once in awhile: "Your turn! Ask me a question and I'll write my answer back to you." I do this about once a semester. It can take awhile to respond to everyone's individual questions, but I love it. It's fun to see what students want to know, and I like being able to share a part of myself with those who want to know more. I've been asked about my favorite book (Harry Potter series), which countries I've visited (lots!), my favorite beverage (iced lattes), why I became a teacher (it's always what I wanted to do), and more. I've also learned that some students will ask weird things, especially middle school students. I remember being asked, "Who was your first kiss?" (like you'd know the person anyway, kid), "Who is your boyfriend?" (again...geez...), and "Who is your favorite student?" The favorite student question gets asked every single year, and I always respond with a standard (but not true—*gasp!*), "I don't have a favorite student!"

Celebrate Birthdays

This is another simple way to show students that you acknowledge them. I had some empty space (a window that looks into a shared area between the two science classrooms) and wanted to fill it with something. I decided to make a "Birthday Window:"

I used some of my budget to order bulletin board cutouts—owls, stars, and frogs. At the beginning of the year, I write the name of each student and their birthday on a randomly selected cutout. I sort the cutouts by birthday month, and then I hang up the cutouts for all the students celebrating each month. At the end of the month,

I give the student their cutout, plus a birthday pencil. It's nothing super fancy or exciting, but the students generally appreciate the recognition and a free pencil.

If you do this, plan ahead for summer birthdays! Our school starts in September and is usually out at the end of May, so my first set of birthdays on the window includes August and September together. In May, I put up the birthdays for May, June, and July. There are always a TON! Make sure you have enough space if you plan to combine birthdays that occur in the summer months. Interestingly, ever since I started doing this, March has historically had the fewest number of birthdays on the window. Huh!

Final Thoughts

You'd be surprised—if you take advantage of talking with students and really getting to know them, most behavior issues will simply fade away. This is not to say that discipline issues will disappear completely— students will still have bad days sometimes, and those bad days might come with outbursts. No one is perfect. However, you will find that the number of issues will significantly decrease, and some of the "worst" students for other teachers will be perfect angels for you—just because you showed them that you care. It's like magic!

Chapter 5: Classroom Management

Tiger tip: *When it comes to classroom management,*
sometimes you need to be a tiger instead of a sloth!

Introduction

The reason I saved this incredibly high-interest topic until this late in the book is because everything I've discussed up to this point helps with classroom management. As you will see, all four areas — policies/procedures, physical organization, active learning strategies, and building relationships — weave together to form the most important aspect of classroom management:

PREVENTION.

I one-hundred percent believe that the most effective type of classroom management is simply predicting situations in which issues will occur, and then working to prevent them. It's as simple as that!

Well, it's not always that simple. I get that. There are still situations where effective management skills will be needed, no matter how hard you work on the back end of things. However, most issues can be stopped before they even start by just planning ahead.

Consider the following situation. Your lesson is going faster than you expected, and you have 15 minutes left. You have no alternative plans, and so you give the students 15 free minutes until the bell rings. You *hope* that they work on other homework or read a book, and you gently suggest they choose one of those options. But then there's the group of students who claim to have no other homework, there are some who say that they are saving homework for study hall (otherwise they'll have nothing to do later), and others never carry an extra book to read. In an instant, that spare time turns into a chance for students to instigate or become disruptive. Of course, this does not happen every time, but it's always a possibility. And once the class is out of control, what do you do? Count down the minutes until the bell rings? Hope that the students magically decide to behave? It's an uncomfortable situation (been there, done that—I know this feeling from my days as an inexperienced long-term sub!), and the best way to deal with it is simply to learn from your mistakes and figure out how to prevent such situations from ever occurring. You can prevent situations by implementing policies and procedures, organizing your physical space, keeping learning active, and building relationships.

How Preventative Measures Make Classroom Management a Breeze

Consider how physical organization can help you with the classroom management in the situation described at the beginning of this chapter. If you make your copies for a unit ahead of time and have them organized (as you saw in Chapter 2), you can grab a related activity or worksheet and give it to the students to complete. They never even have to know that the worksheet was for the next day—it can be your secret! And just like that, the students are busy and less likely to act out.

Let's say that you don't have a worksheet ready, or you have one that really doesn't make sense to start until you have a full class period the next day. Instead, you could hand out student whiteboards (or even scrap paper), and make up review questions off the top of your head. Use questions that correspond with the information/concepts/vocab words that students learned that day, or even throughout the unit so far. You could have students work in groups to collaborate on answers, and you could make a game out of it to increase motivation and participation (consider the "Whiteboard

Game" from Chapter 3- it's very easy to throw together with little-to-no preparation!).

Alternately, you could play a class game of Pictionary that relates to the topic of the day. Divide the class (and your board) in two, and have each side choose a volunteer to draw out the clues. Write down a word or concept, show the volunteers the word, and send the volunteers to their half of the board. The volunteers draw the word or concept, their team guesses the concept, and the team that gets the answer correct wins a point. Repeat with new volunteers. Fifteen minutes will fly by.

If you're not fond of a review game idea, you could keep some extra puzzles, books, or board games on hand, and have students play something when there is extra time to fill. However, if you pull a review aspect into the activity, it's more than just a time buyer—it's an opportunity for reinforcement and learning. And guess what? When students are busy, they don't have time to cause issues! Thus, having an organized classroom and a prepared "what if" plan in place truly is an effective way to combat many classroom management issues.

More Ways that Preventative Measures Help

- Having set policies and procedures for collecting homework reduces wasted time and chaos because students know where to turn in their work and how to do so. Have a task ready for students to do when they've finished turning in their work, such as doing a warm-up problem, so they are *immediately* engaged in the next task as soon as they're back at their desk. Less free time, less issues!

- Having set policies and procedures for students picking up absent work means that students know where to get their things without bothering you while you're trying to get the rest of the group going. When one student sucks up your attention, the others are free to do as they please. If a student tries to ask where to get their work, simply point to your bulletin board or area that they pick information up—just like that, the interaction is over, and you're back to focusing on the class as a whole. Chaos averted!

- In general, having set policies and procedures is one of the best forms of preventative classroom management, as long as you *train students to follow them* (that's key!). Choppy, poorly-transitioned classes breed issues because there are too many spaces for students to cause problems. Students need to practice HOW to request a hall pass, HOW to use a homework pass, HOW to pick up lab equipment, etc. When students have practice in doing these things, there are fewer confused students, and with fewer confused students...you guessed it! Less chaos.

- Having an organized classroom means that students know where to find things. They know which objects they can use without permission (colored pencils, rulers, etc.) and they know which they need to ask for (such as items in your desk drawers). In this way, organization keeps your class running smoothly.

- Having an organized way of directing students, such as by using table numbers, eliminates the chaos and confusion of, "Where do I go?" and the shenanigans that can follow.

- Having an organized way of handing back papers (i.e., having students write their table numbers on their papers so you can quickly sort the papers into groups) means that you waste less time. If you waste less time, you have more time to focus on your class and keep everyone on task. Starting to see a pattern here?

- Keeping learning active is an obvious one. If you keep students moving from task to task within a class period, and if you incorporate variety into your daily routines, most students will not get bored! Bored students are the ones that cause the most issues! Keeping certain routines every day is totally fine, like using "Be Ready to Answer Questions" every time you run a lecture. But spicing things up with a Kahoot (Google it if you don't know what that is!) or POGY cards every once in awhile keeps students guessing what you're going to do tomorrow, and they will be excited to come to your class and will be ready to learn.

- I've saved the most important for last — building relationships. I cannot reiterate how crucial this step is in preventing issues from happening. When you make a point to get to know your students, and when they reach that point of trusting you and feeling safe in your presence, they will being willing to work *with* you because *you know they care.* They will stop working *against* you. Yes, you're still going to have problems here and there. But if a student truly respects you because they know you respect them too, magical things will happen. Guaranteed.

Proximity

So now you have my number one classroom management tool — prevention. But what do you do when the inevitable issue arises? I first utilize *proximity,* and if that doesn't help, I work my way up from there. For me, detention and removal from my classroom are my ultimate last resorts. Start small and save the "big guns" for when you truly need them.

Proximity means that if a student is acting out, I try and shut them down by inching my way closer to them. A student is less likely to continue obnoxious behavior if you're right there next to them; however, I've had the odd student that just doesn't care and will continue regardless. This is extremely rare.

For many students, this proximity is enough of a warning, and you can walk away after 5-10 seconds and be done with it. For others, you may need to stay longer, or loop back more often. And if the behavior continues beyond your best efforts to keep things low-key, you may need to progress to the next step.

Verbal/Written Warning

How you proceed is dictated by the type of student you are working with; this is one of the many reasons why it is important to really know your well. Over the years, I've determined that there are three groups of students:

1) Students who, if you call them out on a behavior in front of their peers, will become extremely embarrassed and traumatized;

2) Students who, if you call them out on a behavior in front of their peers, will become embarrassed enough to stop the behavior,

but they won't be traumatized the rest of their life — just more aware of their actions — so it won't happen again;

3) Students who, if you call them out on a behavior in front of their peers, will become extremely defensive or hungry for attention and will act out more.

If you know your students well enough, you will find that the majority fall into category two and can handle a verbal warning in front of the class such as, "Stop it, or there will be consequences," without breaking into tears or verbal belligerence. However, for students in categories one and three, going with a subtle written warning might be the more effective route than a verbal notification.

When I use this method, I write the student a short, simple note, such as, "The constant talking is really distracting those around you — please stop." I casually walk by the desk of the student and stealthily put the note on their desk, and I watch to make sure they read it. Addressing behavior in this private manner protects the feelings of the extreme-to-embarrass students, and it removes the whole class as an audience for the extremely-defensive-and-jumping-to-action students (which often pushes them to action for the extra attention). For some students, this works. For others, it does not, and I need to continue to dig through my classroom management toolbox for the next step.

Choices

If I need to progress past a simple warning, I will start to offer students choices. I might scoot a chair next to a student and quietly present their options, remove them to the hall to separate the student from their audience, or write down the choices on a note and slide it over. Again, it depends on the student. The set of choices might look something like, "You can either choose to stop this behavior and we won't have any problems, or you will need to go to the office and make up the missed class time later. Remember that I will have to call home if that happens, too. It's your choice."

The student then has a decision to make—they can *choose* to stop the behavior, or they can *choose* to go to the office, make up detention time, and earn a phone call home. This method puts the behavior in the hands of the students and provides a bit of empowerment; most choose to stay.

When I use this method and the student chooses to stop the behavior, I will thank her or him for making the right choice, and then I might provide some options to help the student stay on the right behavioral track for the rest of class. Some students really struggle in that department and need the extra guidance; often, these students *want* to be good, but don't always know how, or they're not quite mature enough to control their behavior yet, even though they have good intentions. So, I might point out a seat they can choose to move to so they're less distracted, or I might tell the student that they can get up and walk around the room if they're feeling frustrated, etc. Many take me up on these offers and create no problems during the rest of the period.

If that still doesn't help, I go to the next step...removal.

Remove to Hall

I try to keep my students in my classes as much as possible, but there are some who just need to be removed from their audience in order to have a decent conversation with them, or to calm them down if they start to get amped up about something. If I must remove a student, I tell the student to wait in the hall for me; I give him or her a chance to cool down, and then I go out to talk to the student when I have a break with the rest of the class. I make sure my class is busy working on something (and I just trust that the class is doing what they're supposed to when I'm outside the room), and then I step out to ask the student about their behavior and what we can do together to help them remedy the situation.

Like all forms of classroom management, this works with some students, but not all. Some will cooperate after this conversation, whereas others won't even look you in the eyes and they will refuse to answer your questions. Some might even walk away from your classroom while you wait for the right moment to step out and talk; I handle this by calling the office and notifying the principal, who takes care of it from there.

While I consider myself very good at classroom management and working with students, there are some students I just can't figure out. All the aforementioned situations have happened to me at some point during my teaching career; don't be surprised if you have some difficult students, too. If big issues happen here and there with just one or two students every couple of years, it doesn't mean that you are a bad teacher. However, if it happens all the time and with many students, I would wonder if your students truly respect you, and if they feel that you care about them.

You need to remember that when it comes to classroom management issues, there might be other factors at play: gender conflict issues (you may have students who listen to male teachers, but not female, or vice-versa), personality conflict issues (you can't get along with everyone), and emotional and behavioral disorders (which a student can't always control). Talk to other teachers who have experience with the student and see what happens in other classes, and that might give you insights as well.

Always remember that with any given student in your classroom, you're only seeing the tip of the iceberg. There is so much under the surface that you cannot (and may not ever) see/understand, and you really shouldn't take such issues personally. My best advice is to work with another teacher who you trust, or to work with a collaborative team to try and get to the root of the issue and to create a solution. Two (or more) heads are better than one!

Detention and Calling Home

Two other tools that I find useful in managing too-late-to-prevent behaviors include giving detention and calling home. Like sending students to the office, these two things cannot be abused, otherwise they lose their power.

I only call home for a small handful of reasons, and always because I've tried working with a student, but it's not helping enough and now I need "back up" from parents/guardians. My reasons for calling home include:

- a student is missing a ton of work and I am concerned about the student falling too far behind,

- a student's attitude/personality/work habits changed and I am worried that something is wrong,

- I removed a student to the office and want the parent to know my side of the story, or

- a student is displaying chronic behavior that has not changed, even though we've tried to work on it together.

Sometimes parents are extremely helpful and support you by providing feedback about what's going on and home, and by having conversations with and/or delivering consequences to the student. Sometimes parents mean well and have good intentions, but their promises are empty. Other parents don't care at all. You may even have parents who refuse to pick up the phone. Whatever the parent/guardian situation, always make that attempt to reach out. Most parents appreciate your efforts, and for the ones who don't, saying that you tried is better than having to admit to an administrator that you did nothing at all if you are confronted about the situation.

On a side note, I highly recommend keeping a "parent contact log" on a sheet of paper or on a document of your computer. Use it to record who you contacted, the date and time, the reason for your call, and the outcome of the call. This way, if you ever need to provide "proof" of making parent contact, or if a parent ever questions something you say, you have a point of reference.

In terms of detention, I know teachers who throw out detentions like a person throwing candy in a parade. This sort of "consequence abuse" means that the students could care less about getting detention time because it's just part of the routine. I only use detention when a student stops responding to proximity and warnings, but they're not causing enough of an issue to get sent to the office. In my class, handing out detention and/or threatening to call home if the behavior does not cease is usually enough to quell the issue.

At my school, you can require students to serve detention in your room (you set up a date/time with them), or you can send the information to the office (length of time owed/reason why owed). If your school has the same options, *please do not choose the latter*. Personally, I see this as a cop-out and as a missed opportunity. There is only one situation in which I will send a detention to the office, which I will explain shortly. Otherwise I ALWAYS make students serve in my room, because I want them to know that they can't easily escape me (mwahahaha!), but also because I also want to make a breakthrough with them. How can you discuss *why* the student is in detention with you and attempt to move forward if they're not even in your room? Many times, students legitimately have no idea why they were given detention if the first place, or the reasoning was lost in translation and they believe it was for something else entirely.

Here is how I advise handling detention. First, choose an amount of time and a consequence that fits the crime. If a student uses a swear word, I might give them a warning at first. However, the second time they do it, they owe me five minutes. Five minutes is annoying! That's not really a lot of time, but it's enough to drive a student crazy if they can't be on their phone for five minutes. Guess what else is annoying? Swearing in school! The time fits the crime.

If a student does something more major, I adjust the time as necessary. I generally never give more than 20 minutes because it starts to become a burden on me. Perhaps that's selfish, but you have to think about yourself, too. If you need to assign longer periods of detention, maybe have the student serve the first 20 with you and the rest in the office, if you can arrange that. Or, split the session over a couple days. However, I like students to serve their detention with me all in one shot so I can try to make a breakthrough without interruption.

After I assign a student detention (either verbally or via note), I give the student a couple minutes to think about the situation. I loop back to talk with them when there is a break in instruction, and I notify the student that I *must* know by the end of class when (date and time) the student will serve the detention. Some students will decide right then and there, whereas others will put off making a decision as long as possible in hopes that you will forget (I make sure to write myself a reminder to check in with them at the end of class!).

In terms of timing, I require students to serve detention on the same day or the day following (in case they need to make bus arrangements) because the longer you wait, the weaker the effect. I write down the date and amount of time on my calendar as soon as the student decides when to serve so I do not forget. I also make sure to reiterate my policy to the student—if they forget to show up for their committed date/time, their detention amount will double. This is where it can get a little out of hand sometimes—if you assign a 20 minute detention and the student forgets to show up, now you have 40 minutes to arrange with the student. This is why I generally never assign more than 20 minutes. Be prepared to find solutions in cases such as these.

If you have trouble trying to get a student to commit to a detention time, call home. I've had a few extremely supportive parents re-arrange schedules and bring the student to school early for detention, and then check in with me later to make sure the student showed up. Teamwork!

Before the student comes in for detention, decide what you're going to "make them do." How about for the student that never gets work done, you sit down with them and help them catch up in your class? Or for the student that likes to talk all hour — make them talk to you nonstop! I'm not kidding! Tell them that if they love to talk, they're going to talk to you the *entire time*...and then sit back and watch (err...listen) as you build a relationship, because now you've started a conversation between yourself and the student.

No matter what you have the student do while serving detention, always, ALWAYS ask them when they arrive if they understand WHY they're there. Sometimes they will admit that they don't, and it becomes a teachable moment in which you can explain your reasoning and ask the student how you can help the student succeed in future situations. Detention should not be "sit and stare at the walls" — what a waste of time. Detention should be time to discuss, learn, and grow.

I'm going to wrap up this section with my favorite detention story. I had a ninth grade student (we'll call him Scott) who just absolutely refused to work during work time one day. I asked him over and over to get on task, but nothing changed. I assigned Scott 20 minutes of detention, told him we'd work on the assignments during that time, and I asked when he could serve it. Scott informed me that he rode the bus both ways and couldn't make arrangements for a ride, so he could *never* serve it. I told him that was interesting (I knew he lived in walking distance of the school) and I said I would be giving his mom a call later on to see what she thought. He left class, I called his mom during my prep, explained the situation, and she said that Scott could definitely walk home from school that day.

The end of the day came, and Scott showed up (his mom got in contact with him before the day had ended). He immediately put his head down on the table; I let him sit there for awhile, even though I wanted him to work, and did my own thing for a couple minutes. Suddenly, out of nowhere, he started a conversation with me. I don't remember the entire dialogue, but I do remember him asking what my favorite subject was in school, and I asked him his. We talked back and forth for a few minutes, and then he pulled out his assignments from class earlier that day and started to work on them while we continued our conversation. When his time was up, Scott left for home; his assignments weren't done at that time, but he made lots of progress. Amazingly, all the assignments came back completed the next day. And the best part? We made tons of connections and built an awesome relationship as a result. Scott was a student who caused problems in many other classes, but from that day forward, he was *never* an issue in my class again. Consider this—if I just made Scott serve detention in the office instead of in my classroom that day, that connection with him would have been *completely* different. Relationships are powerful things.

Removal to the Office

I save office removals for my most uncontrollable students. Again, I would rate my classroom management skills as strong and this rarely happens, but it has. I remove students for of one of two reasons: either they are providing constant disruptions of the learning environment (despite seemingly infinite consequences)

128

and the learning of other students is significantly impacted as a result, or because they are displaying extremely inappropriate behavior (such as preparing to fight). Those are the only two reasons I've ever sent students to the office.

I know teachers who kick students out all the time, and to students in those classes, it's no big deal anymore. They actually *want* to get kicked out because they don't like being in that class anyway. This consequence is to be saved and used with caution so it does not become a joke or an escape.

When I remove a student from my class, my students know that it's a serious endeavor. I call or instant message the office (I prefer the latter, as it's easier to keep a conversation on the "down low") to let the office staff know the student is on the way. I also do this because some students like to wander, and I want to make sure the student follows directions. Then, I send the student out the door and follow up later to make sure the student arrived. In some situations, I might need to call for an escort (the principal, a special education teacher, etc.) — it depends on the behavior and if the student has a behavior plan in place. Finally, when I get the chance, I make a phone call home to explain the situation to the

129

parent/guardian—not only is this the policy at my school, but I feel that it makes sense. I'd rather have the parent or guardian hear my side of the story, rather than just hearing a one-sided story (or no story at all) when the child gets home that night.

All in all, I never let an incident get between my attempt to build a relationship with a student. After any situation, I still work to praise the student when something goes well, talk about non-school things to build that "I still care about you" sense, and discuss the behavior with the student when appropriate to see if progress can be made or if I can support them in any way (such as by moving their seat or keeping them apart from a certain student).

Positive Contacts

Many parents, especially those of "bad kids," are so used to receiving phone calls or emails from school when their student does something wrong. I love turning the tables on a semi-regular basis by calling home to notify parents/guardians of the things their student did *right*—especially those that are branded as "bad kids."

I encourage you to call home for positive things whenever you can—praising kindness from a student who is seen as a bully, expressing excitement for a struggling student who gets a high grade on a test, confirming the positive behavioral changes of a student who just started a new medication, etc. More often than not, parents will be so happy to hear such kind words, and that little bit of praise might be enough to encourage the student to continue the good behavior in the future.

My personal favorite positive contact occurred when I sent an e-mail home to a parent of a student who was supposedly horrendous as an eighth grader. He was so "bad" that he was even sent to alternative school for awhile. This student had obviously grown and matured by the time he reached me as a freshman, and I emailed his mom to let her know what a great job he was doing. I acknowledged that I knew he had issues in the past, but had I not heard of those things, I would have never known! I told her that he was so kind, polite, well-behaved, and hard-working in my class. She emailed me back that she was so excited to hear the news—she was going to print the e-mail and put it in his scrapbook!

Bad Day/Good E-mail

Sometimes, you're going to have really, really, really, bad days as a teacher. On those days, you will have two options: wallow in sorrow and shout to the universe that you're going to quit your job (been there!), or try to shift your thinking to something more positive to make your day just a little bit better.

On one such day, I decided that for the one bad phone call I had to make (a student was horrible that day), I was going to send five positive e-mails home to other parents. I think I actually ended up writing to twelve parents about how wonderful their students were. I thanked the parents for raising kind, respectful, hard-working students, and I sent the messages along. Maybe it doesn't really count as twelve because I wrote to all the parents of my A.P. Biology students, and it was the same e-mail to all twelve people with the student name changed, but hey, it really made me feel better about the day. The task made me think about the "good" students I have and how they significantly outnumbered the "not as good" students, and it made me appreciate how most of my students really wanted to be in school and wanted learn. I didn't totally forget about the horrible situation of the day, but it definitely felt less horrible by the time I went home.

Final thoughts

Classroom management can be such a difficult topic to teach because, more often than not, experience is the best teacher. However, as you've seen here, I strongly believe that by setting up preventative measures — having policies and procedures, staying organized, keeping learning active, and by building relationships — most classroom management issues fade away.

For those issues that do not fade away, having a set plan in place definitely helps. Use proximity and progress from there, depending on what you know about the student. Do they need a verbal or written warning? Can you provide options so they feel like they have a choice? If things escalate, do you assign detention, call home, or send them out of the room? How can you use your relationships with students to make progress? Can you make any positive contacts to continue to build that positivity?

Hopefully the ideas in this section help you modify your classroom management procedures if your current system isn't very effective, or help you design a system if just need to know where to start. Pick and choose and create, then test and revise, and revise some more. Classroom management skills become stronger with practice, and with time, you will have a system that works!

Chapter 6: Miscellaneous Tips and Tricks

Sloth tip: Don't wait until the end of the semester to implement something new. Start tomorrow! Students may resist large changes at first, but eventually, they will settle.

The following pieces of information don't really fit into the previous chapters, but I feel like they are useful ideas to share. Enjoy this random smattering of various tips and tricks!

Scavenger Hunt

On the first or second day of school, I like to orient students to my room using a scavenger hunt (rather than just pointing to the tissue box and saying, "Here's the tissue box!"). I do this activity for a few reasons: first, students are more likely to remember things when they *do* them (rather than just being told), and second, many teachers spend the first day or two of school just going over policies and rules. This means that the students have probably been sitting in these other classes, bored, listening to boring things (important, yes, but boring when that's all you've been listening to the same things over and over all day long). This activity gets students up and moving, talking, laughing, and learning some of my classroom policies (such as where to turn in homework and find absent work) in a subtle manner. I go over the rest of my class rules a day or two later, after all the other teachers are probably done going over theirs. It breaks up the monotony a bit!

For my scavenger hunt, I make up a simple worksheet and print a copy out for each student. If your classroom is one-to-one, you could make up some sort of online form or document to save paper. My scavenger hunt looks like this:

***

Log into your computer. While you wait, answer these questions.

1. What is the puzzle called that I put up every day?
2. Where will you find extra copies of assignments?
3. How many tissue boxes can you find in my room? List their locations.
4. If you are absent, where will you find your assignments when you return?
5. When you turn work in, where will it go?
6. How many pencil sharpeners do I have? Where are they?

When your computer is ready, go to my website, www.fhsmissb.weebly.com.

1. What sort of information will you find on the calendar?
2. Which tab gives you the day-by-day pan for what we're doing in class every day this week?
3. Where will you find the links to assignments if you need to print them at home? There's more than one place!
4. What is my favorite animal?
5. Which country have I visited twice?
6. What sorts of information can be found on the page for your specific class?

***

I give students 10-15 minutes to complete the scavenger hunt, and then we discuss the answers as a group. Again, by finding these answers on their own, students are more likely to remember the information later on down the road. Fun, simple, and effective!

Tissue Boxes

Perhaps you teach at a school where you are supplied with tissue boxes to put around your classroom. My school hands out rolls of toilet paper. I was not a fan — when cold and flu season hits and students need to blow their notes 50 times a minute (or what seems like it, anyway), and all they have is hard, scratchy, yucky toilet paper, I feel sorry for the students. Since I teach on a limited budget (like most teachers) and would prefer to use my money for science supplies rather than tons of tissue boxes, I ask students to bring the boxes in for me.

I remember being required to bring in two boxes of tissues in elementary school, and I guess that's where I got the idea from. My very first year teaching, I told students that if they brought me a tissue box, I would give them five points extra credit (which is a really small amount, but was enough to encourage students to bring me boxes). I let students know that they could bring a maximum of two boxes for 10 points total; I required them to write their name on the bottom in permanent marker (so no one else could try to claim the box as their own) and set it in a designated location before school, during class, or after school. I said they could bring more than two boxes if they wanted, but only two would count for credit, or they could help out someone who might not be able to obtain the boxes themselves (my district is identified by a significant amount of free-and-reduced lunches, so some students live in poverty and might not be able to afford tissues to donate). I set a deadline of a week and watched the boxes flow into my room!

The first time I did this, I obtained about 150 boxes in one week. I'm lucky that my room has a lot of storage space, otherwise I would have had some issues! That first set of tissues lasted me about three or four years before I had to repeat the process and request more boxes!

Every time I need more tissues and make the request/extra credit bribe, students bring me boxes without even thinking twice. All I have to do is remind them about the scratchy toilet paper of other classrooms, and they bring boxes so they can blow their noses in luxury when they are in my class. Sometimes I even have

140

students pop in to grab a tissue during passing time, and they aren't even in any of my classes! They just know that my room has the best nose care in school!

Sub Plans

Unfortunately, being gone is often more work than simply being in school. I hate the amount of preparation and catch-up that having a substitute teacher entails, but sometimes you just get sick, or you have a great workshop to attend, or you have a personal/family issue that you can't avoid. To be ready for all situations, make sure you have two kinds of sub plans ready: emergency plans and a ready-to-use template for non-emergency plans.

If you've ever subbed before, you know that it is a HARD job. You also know (or can imagine, if you haven't been a sub before) that vague sub plans are TERRIBLE for the substitute teacher to deal with — unless they are a veteran sub for your school, they will probably be overwhelmed by many things, such as the new environment, unfamiliar students of varying cooperation levels, the task trying to find your seating charts/discipline plan/bell schedules, etc. If your plans are unclear or come up short, your substitute might get confused, frustrated, and/or do things you didn't plan

141

(or carry out your plans the wrong way). Thus, it is imperative that you write clear, specific, and easy-to-follow sub plans, and that you provide your subs with the other important information that they might need to make it through the day.

I keep my sub plans in a bright, yellow folder. The folder is clearly marked "sub plans" and is visible from across the room. I do this because you can't always plan for an absence — if I get really sick and have to call in at 5am, there's no way I'm commuting half an hour to school to pull out my folder and set items on the front desk for the substitute teacher. Instead, I tell my principal (or teacher next door) where my folder is, and they can easily pull it out for me and have it ready to go.

In my sub folder, I label the pockets with what's on each side so it's easier to find information. I include:

- ✓ **My class lists.** At the bottom of each class list, I write down the names of two girls and two boys that are helpful/very nice students.

- ✓ **The school bell schedules.**

✓ **Detention slips**, which I personally don't use, but sometimes it's nice for a sub to have a place to document incidents if they feel detention is necessary.

✓ **Fire drill, tornado, and active shooter emergency information**.

✓ **How to dial other rooms on my phone, how to dial outside of school, and a list of phone extensions.**

✓ **My emergency sub plan sheet**. This sheet always stays in the folder, whether I have a planned sub or not. If my sub is planned, I include a separate sheet with specifics for the day.

Emergency plans are *so* important for the days you do not expect to be absent. On the emergency plan sheet, I reference: how to access the announcements, how to take attendance, how to input attendance into the computer, my music policy, my cell phone policy, information about my hall pass policy (and not to worry about tracking the passes), and how to contact me. I also

143

have very general sub plans — basically, to give students a study hall or a movie day (and I indicate the location of my movies).

For my regular sub plans, I created a template so I can easily use the same format over and over. Again, it is super important that you are as clear and specific as possible in your instructions. However, you also need to keep in mind the "overwhelm" factor. If your plans are so densely packed with instructions in huge paragraphs and blocks of information, the substitute teacher might experience sensory overload and miss some information. Thus, I try to make use of bullets and shorter sentences/statements as much as possible.

On my sub plans, I include information about how to log into my computer (Hint! If you are comfortable with the idea, write the login info on the bottom of a tissue box near your computer and make reference to it in your plans! Students never know it's there!), the location of important items (like seating charts), and other relevant information (for instance, if it's a test, which students will leave to take it in the special education room). It doesn't hurt to also clarify your (or the school's) cell phone policy so the substitute knows how to handle mobile devices.

What follows is an example of my sub plans for one day. Remember, I teach at a small school and have lots of classes to prepare for, so I have a lot of different instructions to give. If you only teach two classes, your sub plans will be so much easier to write! As you read, note the level of specificity that I include, yet how I try to break up the information with bullets to decrease the overwhelm factor. Feel free to copy my format if it works for you!

***

Sub Plans: Danielle Carlson, Room 503

NOTES

- To log in to my computer, use the username/password written on the bottom of the Kleenex box by my table. My Skyward login is also located there.

    o **When you log in to my computer, a weird screen will appear upon startup that has some big boxes in the center.** You have to click the gray "x" at the bottom right corner (might be partially hidden near the time area) to get to my regular desktop background.

    o **When you turn on the SmartTV for the first time,** you will probably see a black screen- it's the table by my desk! The Doc cam automatically turns on first for some weird reason. Go over to the Doc cam and hit the button with the gold arrow by it. This will switch the view on the front board to the computer instead of the doc cam.

- **_If someone is absent, PLEASE ALSO write their name in the small calendar next to the seating chart._** This helps me out a LOT.

- Aids and assistants:
    - 3rd hr: Maggie (special education aide)
    - 4th hr: Katie (student assistant)

1st hour- Anat & Phys-

- Preparatory things:
    - Project the slide that tells them what is going on today. This is found on my right-hand monitor up in the left corner (says "Class Today- Shortcut"). This should be on the board when they walk in the room. Hit F5 at the top of the keyboard to put in presentation mode.

    - Announcements are at 8:05. Click "announcements" on the top right corner of the slide once it is in presentation mode. Make sure the computer volume is up and drag the screen over to the right monitor.

- Hand back papers.

- If Sam is gone, please send Alex a message. I haven't seen Sam in weeks, so don't expect to see him.

- They have a test today. Sarah V. might come early to grab it (before class starts) and head to the special education room to take it- that is fine.
    - They need to spread out as much as possible and put up binder blockers. This is routine, so they should know what to do when you tell them.
    - They turn in the test when it is done. Feel free to grade the multiple choice for me! I will do the rest later.

2nd hour- AP Bio- Remember to switch the slide.

- Hand back papers.

146

- They have a quiz first. They get a SIMPLE calculator, an equation sheet (please hand them a fresh one), and the quiz.

- When done, they have a work day and know what to do. Remind them that I'd like the Deep Dive worksheet by the end of class on Friday.

3rd hour- Applied STEM- Remember to switch the slide.

- Gold data sheets are due. Since I'm not here today, lucky them- as long as I get it by the end of class, that's fine. All of the papers for a table need to be turned in **together** and paper clipped. I already have all the papers from tables 1 (numbers hanging above the tables), 3, and 5. The other groups need to turn in their papers as a group to you, and I will grade them later.

- Max was gone yesterday. Please direct him to the board by the door (I know he won't go there on his own) and he needs to get his gold sheet. Since he was gone yesterday and his group already handed papers in, he needs to complete it on his own and turn in individually.

- Since I'm not there to intro the new project, they get a free day. You can either give them a study hall, or put on a science video from the cabinet closest to the goggle cabinet…feel free to pick one. You could also, through Chrome, go to hulu.com and choose my profile. You shouldn't have to log in. If you choose a video, I will probably have to finish it tomorrow (which is totally fine)- just let me know which one it is and at what time I should pick it up on Friday.

4th, 5th, 6th hr- Biology- Switch the slide.

- Return any work. Make sure all absent kids from yesterday get their work off the board.

- Tell them that they will do the graph prompt shortly, but you have some reminders to give them first.
  - Once they finish the graph prompt, they need to work on their two worksheets. LO4 worksheet is due TOMORROW at the beginning of class, and LO5 is due Monday. They will NOT have time in class tomorrow to work on either.

- Tell them that there is extra credit on the side table by the birthday window. If they choose to do it, it's due Tues 2-7. It's also in Classroom; they can print it from there as well.

- Then, all students will complete the graph prompt. This is for my Educator Effectiveness and should be treated like a quiz. Tell the students to:
  - Remember what they've lost points for in the past and make a conscious effort to NOT make those mistakes again.
  - Try their best!
  - Keep their eyes on their own papers and turn it upside-down when done. That's your cue to pick it up.
  - Work on their worksheets when done.

Lunch

<u>RTI</u>- It's an ACT prep group. They need to:

- Log in to albert.io
- I assigned three question sets. They should choose one to complete. If they finish, they should pick another.
- If they have login issues or trouble finding the assignment, they can work with a partner on one Chromebook.

7th hour- Prep (finally, right?!?!)

8th hour- A&P – Same as 1st hour. Feel free to skip the announcements.

Thank you! If you need anything, feel free to text me at xxx-xxx-xxxx or call. I'm just at CESA today and will have my phone on me all day.

- Danielle

****

148

Using Visuals

Students (and adults!) often understand things better with a visual. The idea for using visuals is not my own—I learned about this concept by reading <u>Picture This!,</u> by Rick Smith. After reading the book, I wondered why I hadn't thought of using visuals more often—it was such a "duh!" moment. Visuals are easy to create and they save (what feels like) hours of repeating instructions—just take a picture, throw it into a slideshow or photo editing program to add words, print, post, and point to it as needed. Boom! Done.

Most of my visual rubrics are for lab activities. Smith's book gives lots of good ideas for other classroom uses (many of which are great for elementary and middle school teachers). I love them for explaining how to do a tough measurement:

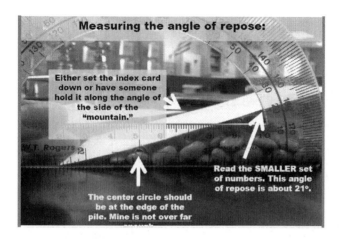

Measuring the angle of repose:

Either set the index card down or have someone hold it along the angle of the side of the "mountain."

Read the SMALLER set of numbers. This angle of repose is about 21°.

The center circle should be at the edge of the pile. Mine is not over far

I especially love these for showing students what their lab table needs to look like before they leave:

Clean graduated cylinder

No cornstarch on table

Dry, clean beaker

Your table should be set up like this.

Spoon clean and in beaker

There are tons of other ways to use these visuals — the options are endless! I don't know how I went so long without using them in the first place! I highly recommend checking out Rick Smith's book for more information.

Rebus Puzzle

I borrowed this idea from my cooperating teacher while student teaching because I saw how much students loved solving puzzles. It took me awhile to figure out a system that minimized students running into the room and immediately shouting the answer at the top of their lungs, ruining the puzzle for everyone else. After some trial and error, I created a "game" of sorts that works for me.

I bought three small whiteboards, as shown in my picture above, because I had no room on my main board. The top board gets a new "Rebus Puzzle" each day (unless a puzzle can't be solved; more on that later). I get my puzzles from the book shown at the bottom of the picture — <u>Thinklers</u>, by Kevin Brougher. I also find some puzzles online. The bottom left board hosts the daily winner, and the bottom right board hosts the weekly winner.

When students walk into my room, most look at the puzzle right away. I even have students come in to solve the puzzle who aren't even in my classes anymore! If they think they know the answer, participants write the answer on a piece of scrap paper with their name (I keep a little blue basket with a bunch of paper in it, plus a pencil on a string...otherwise the pencil accidentally walks away!). The participants then put the guess in the "rebus puzzle guesses" jar, which is just a large plastic container with a lid and a hole in the lid. I have a little sign near the jar (it's under the book in my picture) that reminds students that if they forget to put their name on the slip, they can't win because I don't know whose guess is whose.

At the end of the day, I shake up all the guesses and randomly select one. I read the answer, and if it is incorrect, I go to the next guess, and so on. The first person with the correct answer is the "daily winner," and their name goes on the left-hand board. Students love seeing their name up there when they win! I save the slip for each daily winner (so I can choose the weekly winner—explained shortly), put up a new puzzle, and write the answer for the old puzzle on the large board. If no one gets the puzzle for the day (I like to throw in some really difficult ones now and then), I leave the puzzle up for another day, but I write a hint on the board near the puzzle. In that situation, the daily winner is listed as "none" and everyone gets a second chance at guessing.

At the end of the week, I throw the five winning slips for the week into the jar and choose one for the weekly winner. The weekly winner gets a pencil on Monday that says "student of the week." It's nothing crazy-amazing, but it's enough to make students excited to win! They also just like seeing their name up on the board—that recognition is often exciting enough!

A confession: sometimes I fudge the results. If the same person wins on Monday and Tuesday, I just pick a new person for Tuesday. Some students are *extremely* good at these puzzles and could probably win every day, but I like to give other students a chance. The only exception to this rule is when it comes to really hard puzzles. Let's say that Shawna won on Monday, and on

154

Tuesday, she's the only person to guess the puzzle correctly. I'll let her win on that second day just because she was the only person to guess and get it correct.

Something to watch out for: overzealous students. I once had a middle school student who wanted to win so badly that he put in 23 guesses (without me noticing him put all those guesses in the container!). I would have never caught on, except that day, I picked his guess first, and it was wrong. So I picked another one, and it was the same student with the same guess. I was suspicious, and went through the rest of the slips, and counted 23 sheets of scrap paper in his name. I had to laugh for the sake of his creativity (it *was* pretty funny), but I only let each student guess once out of fairness for others. His consequence — he wasn't allowed to guess the puzzle for 23 days. I thought that was pretty funny, too.

Keep a Running List!!!

I HIGHLY recommend that you start a running list of everything you do as a teacher — start right now if you don't have one going already. It doesn't have to be fancy, and it doesn't even have to be digital. However, I love having a Google Doc that I can update from anywhere and at any time, and I can move things and group them with a click of a mouse. You want to include the following items on this list:

- Workshops/trainings you attend — their name, location, date, and if you receive any credits for it (and the institution they come from).
- Workshops you present at — name, location, date.
- Graduate courses you take — name of the class, the school it is through, semester/year of the class, credits received.
- Memberships that you possess — name of organization, dates active, ID number.
- Grants and awards you've received — name of grant/award, amount of grant/award, date received.
- Student teachers you've worked with — name, which quarter(s) they were with you, school year.
- Anything else that you feel is important to make note of (clubs, coaching, etc.).

Keeping this list has assisted me greatly. It has helped me maintain my resume, which I've used for job applications and award applications (like PAEMST), it has helped me keep track of my credits so I can make sure I move on the pay scale when I'm supposed to, it has helped me remember when I've worked with certain student teachers for recommendation letters years down the road, and more. I've referenced my list so many times since I started teaching, and if I didn't have that file on my computer, I would have had a heck of a time digging in old folders and finding online registration confirmations for various pieces of paperwork. Save yourself the hassle!

Organizing Units and Lessons on the Computer

If you organize your files on your computer, it will be a lot easier to find items when you need them. I utilize numbers in file folders to "force" files into an order that make sense to me (instead of alphabetically). If you use Google Drive, make sure you put a zero in front of your single digit numbers (01, 02, 03... instead of 1, 2, 3...) otherwise 10 will actually end up at the top of your list when you sort your files by name. I personally like to keep my folders for content/classes together, and then my important (but not class-related) information at the top by starting the folder with a double zero (00):

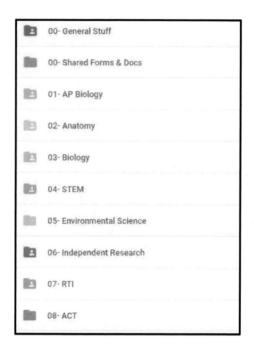

I use the same system within my unit folders—I use numbers at the beginning of file names to force the order there, too. I generally don't use the zeros at the beginning because I tend to stay below nine:

```
Lab Practical
Test
0- Combo notes packet
1- Epithelial Tissues worksheet
2- Epithelial Tissues Webquest
3- Epithelial slides lab
4- Epith and conn rev wkst
5- CT M and N lab
6- Tissue review pkt
6.5- Histology sort cards
7- membranes worksheet
8- histo review sheet
PPT 1- Intro, Epithelium
PPT 2- Types of epithelial tissues- NEARP...
PPT 2- Types of epithelial tissues
PPT 3- Connective Tissue
PPT 4 Review- Epith and conn tssu POGY
PPT 5- muscle and nervous tissue notes
PPT 6- membranes, diseases, aging
PPT 7- Lab Practical Review
PPT 7- Practical info
PSR Histo 1
PSR Histo 2
```

Here is a different numbering system that you could also use to sort files:

- 6.0a Unit 6 Inspiration
- 6.1 Type of Engineering Sign Up
- 6.1 Types of Engineering
- 6.2 Intro to Bridges
- 6.3 Bridge Types and Forces Worksheet
- 6.3 Bridge Types and Forces Worksheet
- 6.3a- Exploring Bridge Forces- Online_I
- 6.3b- Exploring Bridge Forces Lab
- 6.4- Exploring Bridge Components
- 6.5 How the Tallest Bridge on Earth wa
- 6.6 Bridge Costs- PRINT
- 6.6 cost estimation key
- 6.7 Summary So Far
- 6.8 New Team Team Building
- 6.9 Bridge Contest
- Bridge results

Find what works for you and go with it! I can't imagine having a folder of scrambled documents and trying to find the exact one I'm looking for in a decent amount of time. My system is set up so the files are in the order that I use them throughout any given unit. If it's your first year teaching, it might not be possible for you to have an organized system just yet, but you can certainly start to put things in order as you create them and modify numbers in the future/as needed.

160

Backing Up Your Files Every Year

My final tip: if your hard work isn't saved on a cloud out in internet land somewhere, buy an external hard drive or flash drive to save backups of everything you do. I suggest this for two reasons: first, you never know when your computer is going to die. It always happens at the worst possible moment, and it's such a horrible feeling to lose all your hard work. So, back up your files at the end of the school year, and if possible, even more often than that as a "just in case." The second is because you never know when you'll want a file that you made years ago but stopped using. I've had this happen more than once!

At the end of the school year, I make a folder on my hard drive for that school year (let's say 2015-2016). I copy and paste ALL of my teaching files into the folder, leaving the original files on my school computer so I can modify, add, delete, and build off what I did the previous year. At the end of the next school year, I plug in my hard drive, make a new folder (this time it would be 2016-2017), copy all of my files into the folder, and leave the originals for modification the next year.

My external hard drive is huge, so it doesn't matter that I have ALL of my files from the past however many years saved on it. I love this system because it keeps an evolution of my classes on hand, and when I want that old activity from 2010, I can go back and find it. Or, if I've accidentally deleted some file (it's happened), I don't panic because I know that I can go into the folder for last year on my hard drive, copy it over onto my computer, and go from there.

I'll be the first to admit that I'm a bit paranoid about losing my files, so I actually have two external hard drives (they're not too expensive) and keep one at home and one at school...just in case! If your files are online and in "the cloud," you don't really have to worry about them getting lost—but you won't be able to go back and recover old documents from years back if you're always working within the same folders year after year and deleting things. In this case, I suggest making a folder called "Old Files" or "Unused." That way, you never delete the activities and files you've created, and if you need the files in the future, you will know exactly where they are.

Chapter 7: Helpful Resources

Sloth tip: There are so many great books out there!
When you find fantastic reads, be sure to share them
with your teacher friends!

These are some of my favorite resources that I have used to improve my teaching methods. I have read each one and highly recommend them all! Remember to check with your library to see if they have the books you are interested in (or if they can get them from interlibrary loan). This will save you some money!

My top five favorite resources (in no particular order):

- Why Didn't I Learn This in College? Second Edition by Paula Rutherford (Feb. 1, 2009)
- 25 Quick Formative Assessments for a Differentiated Classroom: Easy, Low-Prep Assessments That Help You Pinpoint...(2nd ed.) by Judith Dodge (Jun. 17, 2017)
- Active Learning: 101 Strategies to Teach Any Subject by Mel Silberman (Mar. 1, 1996)
- Great Group Games: 175 Boredom-Busting, Zero-Prep Team Builders for All Ages by Susan Ragsdale and Ann Saylor (Jul. 1, 2007)
- Thinklers! A Collection of Brain Ticklers by Kevin Brougher and Missing Piece Press (Nov. 1, 2000)

Books about differentiation, variety, and assessments:

- Differentiating Instruction in the Regular Classroom: How to Reach and Teach All Learners Grades 3-12 by Diane Heacox Ed.D. (Nov. 15, 2002)

- Differentiating Instruction with Menus: Science (Grades 6-8) by Laurie Westphal (May 1, 2009) *She has a series of books- various subjects, various grade levels.

- Differentiation: From Planning to Practice, Grades 6-12 by Rick Wormeli (Oct. 21, 2007)

- Summarization in Any Subject: 50 Techniques to Improve Student Learning by Rick Wormeli (Dec. 1, 2004)

- Teaching Outside the Box: How to Grab Your Students by Their Brains, 3rd ed. by LouAnne Johnson (Sept. 15, 2015)

- Differentiating Instruction in the Regular Classroom: How to Reach and Teach All Learners Grades 3-12 by Diane Heacox Ed.D. (Nov. 15, 2002)

- Picture This! Visuals and Rubrics to Teach Procedures, Save Your Voice, and Love Your Students by Rick Smith (2011)

- Conscious Classroom Management: Unlocking the Secrets of Great Teaching by Rick Smith (Sept. 30, 2004)

- Meet Me in the Middle: Becoming an Accomplished Middle Level Teacher by Rick Wormeli (Sept. 5, 2001)

Science-specific teaching resources

- The Sourcebook for Teaching Science, Grades 6-12: Strategies, Activities, and Instructional Resources by Norman Herr (Aug. 11, 2008)

- Anatomy & Physiology Coloring Workbook: A Complete Study Guide (12th Edition) by Elaine N. Marieb and Simone Brito (Jan. 13, 2017)

- The Complete Human Body (Book & DVD-ROM) by DK Publishing, Dr. Alice Roberts and Medi-Mation (Aug. 16, 2010) *this book is sometimes better than my classroom textbook! Less expensive too.*

- Science Formative Assessment, Volume 1: 75 Practical Strategies for Linking Assessment, Instruction, and Learning by Page D. Keeley (Oct. 15, 2015)

- It's Debatable! Using Socioscientific Issues to Develop Scientific Literacy K-12 by Dana L. Zeidler and Sami Kahn (Feb. 26, 2014)

- Teaching for Conceptual Understanding in Science by Richard Konicek-Moran and Page D. Keeley (Mar. 1, 2015)

- Argument-Driven Inquiry in Biology: Lab Investigations for Grades 9-12, by Victor Sampson, Patrick Enderle, Leeanne Gleim, Jonathon Grooms, Melanie Hester, Sherry Southerland, and Kristin Wilson (May 15, 2014)

Closing

Well, that's it. That's all I know...for now. My knowledge as a teacher is constantly growing with experience and collaboration, so I'm sure that someday, I'll be able to come out with another edition of this book because I'll have new content to add. One of the best things about teaching is the chance to be a lifelong learner—new knowledge is so exciting and fun to incorporate into what you already know and do!

Best of luck to you in your teaching career, whether it's your first year or your tenth, somewhere between or somewhere beyond—and I hope that you found some useful information in this book that will make your year smoother, easier, and, of course, less stressful.

Take care!

Danielle Carlson

Acknowledgements

First, I would like to thank all my mentors, co-workers, teacher friends, non-teacher friends, current and former students, and *my* teachers as a student. All of these have people helped mold me into who I am as a teacher and have given me so many great ideas, whether or not they realized it! Also, an extra special thanks to all my volunteer editors and feedback-providers. This book would be full of errors without you!

Second, a huge, ginormous, fantastic thank you to my husband, Aaron, who listens to me talk about how much I love my job, how much I hate my job, how overwhelmed I am, how elated I am, how I'm going to get a new career, how I'm going to stay in my career, the anger welling up in me because of a student, the amazing breakthrough I had with a student, and many other opposing comments that spew from my mouth on any given day of any given week. He lets me cry out my frustrations and just listens, and he constantly reminds me that everything is going to be okay (because it always turns out just fine). He makes me stop working sometimes to go for walks, work out, or just breathe…and without him, I'd be a huge mess. He is my anchor. He is also an amazing artist, as he illustrated all the pictures in this book. He is a remarkable person as a whole, and I cannot thank him enough for just being who he is...and for putting up with my craziness and constant shenanigans. That man deserves an award. He's also very talented, as you can see from his sloth (and tiger) drawings!

Third, a giant thank you goes out to my parents. I am so blessed to have parents who care so much, as I see students with parents who care so little and it breaks my heart. I am so lucky to have parents who value education so highly and who always pushed me (but not too crazy-hard) to be my best. My earliest memories include my parents reading to us as children, playing rhyming and vocabulary games sporadically, and buying us reading/writing workbooks to do over summer vacation while we were growing up (*ugh!!!*). My parents have supported me through every decision I've made, providing counsel but not judgement. They've watched me grow as a teacher, often telling me to stop putting so much time into my job because I give 2000% and need to take some time for myself (sigh, I *know*....they're right. Parents are always right). I have also stolen many teaching ideas from my father, who is a successful mentor, teacher, and workshop leader in the areas of law enforcement and loss protection. Thanks, Dad!

Fourth, I'd like to thank my siblings, who sat through endless hours of "pretend school" when we were kids, and I was probably always the teacher. They were good sports and faithfully did the homework that I assigned from discontinued workbooks and textbooks. I'm pretty sure I gave them quizzes and tests, too, just because I liked grading papers. Those are my first memories of wanting to be a teacher, and I'm grateful that they let me boss them around so much.

Finally, I'd like to thank my dog, Tessa. That's probably weird, seeing as she can't read and will never know that I'm writing this for her, but oh well. I'm forever grateful for the puppy dog look that says, "Walk me instead of doing work!" because it makes me get up and take a break; for getting me through some pretty rough periods in both my teaching career and my life (before my husband was in the picture to be my shoulder to cry on); and for the best morning snuggles and creating the "comfort vortex" that makes me want to stay in bed all day, which is extremely counterproductive for writing books and doing work, but it's so relaxing and makes me very happy!

65717308R00098

Made in the USA
San Bernardino, CA
04 January 2018